Yale Near Eastern Researches, 3

Enheduanna on a limestone disc from Ur (restored)

The Exaltation
of Inanna

BY WILLIAM W. HALLO
AND J. J. A. VAN DIJK

New Haven and London
Yale University Press
1968

Acknowledgments

This study in its present form is my responsibility, but only coauthorship can do justice to the debt it owes to Dr. van Dijk for the patient and extended collaboration he bestowed on it at every stage. My thanks are further due, in the first instance, to Samuel Noah Kramer, who not only suggested the collaboration, but who also provided me with numerous duplicates in copy, cast, or original form, as well as with photographs and with opportunities to collate the previously published material. I am grateful, too, to Thorkild Jacobsen for ceding his publication rights to duplicates from the 3NT group of Nippur texts, to K. R. Veenhof (Leiden) for permission to utilize a text from the A. Smit Collection, and to Å. Sjöberg for generously relinquishing his prior interest in the present text. Finally, it is a pleasure to record here the grants which, during 1965-66, supported the travel and research needed to bring this project to a conclusion: a Yale University Senior Faculty Fellowship and a John Simon Guggenheim Memorial Foundation Fellowship.

W.W.H.

Contents

List of Plates

CHAPTER 1

Enheduanna: Her Life and Works

Cuneiform literature has long been stigmatized as anonymous, or at best pseudonymous, and this in marked contrast to the literature of the ancient world generally, which placed a high value on attribution, authentic or merely traditional, whether we look at Egyptian literature, or Hittite, Canaanite, Hebrew, or Greek. By the same token, Mesopotamia plays almost no role in the standard histories of autobiography, where it is represented solely by royal inscriptions.[1] And yet this judgment has recently had to be revised. It is true that the colophons of Sumerian and Akkadian literary series—which correspond to the title pages of a modern book—fail to mention authors' names.[2] But this omission is made good in other ways, most notably by separate lists of authors' names in combination either with the kings they served (by way of dating them)[3] or with the works which, rightly or wrongly, were attributed to them;[4] in other cases the text of the composition revealed, in more or less open form, the name of the author.[5]

This last practice can no longer be said to be a late phenomenon in Mesopotamian literature. For at or near the very beginning of classical Sumerian literature, we can now discern a corpus of poetry of the very first rank which not only reveals its author's name, but delineates that author for us in truly autobiographical fashion. In the person of Enheduanna, we are confronted by a woman who was at once princess, priestess, and poetess, a personality who set standards in all three of her roles for many succeeding centuries, and whose merits were recognized, in singularly Mesopotamian fashion, long after.

The sources for Enheduanna's remarkable career are of three kinds: historical, archaeological, and literary. The contemporary inscriptions from Ur, now conveniently listed by I. J. Gelb[6] and H. Hirsch,[7] show her to have

1. Cf. e.g. Georg Misch, *Geschichte der Autobiographie* (3rd ed. 1949), pp. 36–46.
2. But see below, p. 3.
3. Cf. J. J. A. van Dijk, *UVB*, *18* (1962), 44–52.
4. W. G. Lambert, *JCS*, *16* (1962), 59–77.
5. W. W. Hallo, *Israel Exploration Journal*, *12* (1962), 14–16.
6. *MAD*, *2* (2nd ed. 1961), 194.
7. *AfO*, *20* (1963), 9 sub 2; cf. also E. Sollberger, *AfO*, *17* (1954–56), 26, nn. 90–93.

been the daughter of Sargon and high priestess (en) of the moongod Nanna of Ur. As such she stands at the head of a long succession of princely holders of this office, all of whom are now known until the end of the reign of Rim-Sin some five centuries later.[8] We know from these inscriptions that she functioned in the reign of her nephew Naram-Sin, but it is probable that she had already assumed her office in the lifetime of her father Sargon[9] at least a quarter of a century earlier, for long terms of office were the rule rather than the exception for the high priestess of Nanna. The functions of the office have been described by Boehl, Gadd, and others[10] and will occupy us again later.

The archaeological record for Enheduanna is unique. The two seals mentioning her name[11] are designed in classical Akkadian style. According to Boehmer,[12] they show close affinities to the seals of Lugalanda and Urukagina and thus date from the very beginning of the Akkad period. This is a factor to remember when attempting a more precise dating of her "reign." The seal impression's style, on the other hand, is held unthinkable in the early Akkadian period by Boehmer.[13] Does it date from her old age?

Of even greater interest is the fragmentary disc from Ur[14] inscribed with her name and showing the high priestess herself flanked by three of her retainers.[15] According to the excavator, "this stone has been smashed and deliberately defaced."[16] Perhaps this happened in the course of Enheduanna's expulsion from Ur as reconstructed below. Her face, however, is well preserved. It is shown in profile, and is far from stylized. She is shown wearing the tiara appropriate to her priestly office (see l. 107). The nose is sharply aquiline, the features intent and intelligent, and the bearing determined and individualistic.

Most impressive of all, however, is the literary record.[17] We still do not know the full extent of Enheduanna's literary œuvre, but so strong is the

8. Sollberger, 23–29; cf. also his table, ibid., pp. 45 f. On the question of the missing en names, if any, see Hallo, "Gutium" in *RLA 3* (in press).

9. See below, pp. 2 f. and 6 ff.

10. F. M. Th. de Liagre Boehl, *Symbolae Koschaker* (1939), pp. 151–78 = *Opera Minora* (1953), pp. 174–87 and pp. 490–93; C. J. Gadd, *Iraq, 13* (1951), 27–39. Cf. also H. H. Figulla, *Iraq, 15* (1953), 97–104, 188–92.

11. Above, notes 6 and 7.

12. Moortgat AV (1964), pp. 43 f., and Pl. 10:1–5.

13. Ibid.; cf. Boehmer, *Die Entwicklung der Glyptik . . . (= Untersuchungen zur Assyriologie, 4,* 1965), 25 and n. 105.

14. See the frontispiece for its restoration.

15. U. 6612 = CBS 16665. For the inscription, see *UET* 1:23; for a photograph of the unrestored piece, see C. L. Woolley, *UE, 4* (1955–56), Pl. 41d; for earlier photographs and literature, cf. Hirsch, *AfO, 20* (1963), n. 77.

16. Woolley, *UE, 4,* 49.

17. Cf. already A. Falkenstein, *RA, 52* (1958), 129–31, and *ZA, 52* (1957), 65, n. 1, whose insights anticipated many of the conclusions reached below.

stamp of her style and her convictions in the poems that can definitely be attributed to her, that it may one day be possible to detect her authorship also in other, less well-preserved pieces.[18] For the present we can say with some assurance that the great cycle of hymns to the temples of Sumer and Akkad (é-u₄-nir), a major piece of Mesopotamian theology, is, on the authority of its own colophon, from her hand.[19] The poem in-nin me-huš-a, generally referred to as the "Myth of Inanna and Ebih," does not mention Enheduanna by name in the portions so far published.[20] Yet it almost certainly fits into her cycle of hymns to Inanna, and not only stylistically: its main theme, the revolt of Ebih (i.e. Jebel Hamrin)[21] presumably against Naram-Sin, is alluded to also in another hymn of praise (zà-mí) to Inanna, known from its incipit as in-nin šà-gu₅-ra. In this hymn, Inanna's conquest of Ebih is referred to as the parade example of the goddess' warlike prowess in one brief couplet (ll. 109 f.) which virtually presupposes the text of "Inanna and Ebih."[22] In it, Enheduanna speaks in the first person at least once,[23] and its principal theme is the acknowledgment of Inanna's jurisdiction, her omnipresent and omnipotent role in human affairs, under the motto of "'Tis thine, oh Inanna" (ᵈinanna za-(a-) kam = ku-(um-)ma eštar).

There can be little doubt that this is simply a hymnic expansion of the same acknowledgment that, according to the historical tradition, marked Sargon's successful suppression of the general rebellion late in his reign. The three accounts of this rebellion in the chronographic literature[24] show that, in Sargon's old age (i-na ši-bu-ti-šu), all the countries revolted against him and besieged him in the city of Akkad, but that Sargon broke the siege and inflicted

18. [Since this was written, I. Bernhardt and S. N. Kramer have published another Enheduanna-text with important points of contact with our own, in *TMH* n. F. 4:7 ll. 107–68; cf. especially below, Chap. 5, n. 30.]

19. See the forthcoming edition by A. Sjöberg, *TCS* 3.

20. Cf., in addition to the texts listed by M. Lambert, *RA, 55* (1961), 56, No. 20, and *56* (1962), 214, especially *UET* 6/1:12–17.

21. For this identification, cf. already E. Weidner, *AfO, 9* (1933–34), 46, nn. 35–38, and F. Thureau-Dagin, *RA, 31* (1934), 84–86; more recently: E. Ebeling, *RLA, 2* (1938), s.v. Ebih; Gelb, *AJSL, 55* (1938), 67 f.; Falkenstein, *CRRAI, 2* (1951), 15 f.; D. O. Edzard, *ZZB* (1957), p. 35, n. 152; E. Reiner, *RA, 57* (1963), 173 f.

22. Cf. *Belleten, 16* (1952), 354, Pl. lxiii:iii 18 f.

23. Ibid., Pl. lxv, v 19 = line 215.

24. Two of these accounts are preserved in the form of historic extispicy reports (amūt[EŠ]ᵘᵗ LUGAL.GI.NA), one neo-Assyrian (L. W. King, *Chronicles Concerning Early Babylonian Kings, 2* [1907], 6, ll. 11–13) and the other neo-Babylonian (ibid., pp. 41 f., ll. 5–11), the third in a chronicle (ibid., p. 6, ll. 11–13) which is probably ultimately dependent on the mantic tradition; cf. J. J. Finkelstein, *PAPhS, 107* (1963), 469 and n. 34. For the general reliability of historical data preserved in or through the omen literature, cf. ibid., pp. 462 f. and A. Goetze, *JCS, 1* (1947), 253–65. See also H. G. Güterbock, *ZA, 42* (1934), 59.

a decisive defeat on the rebels, who thereupon acknowledged Ištar (*ku-um* $^d E š_4$-*dar il-su-ú*).

These events, and their poetic expression, are in turn presupposed by the hymn edited below. This refers to the "'Tis thine" of Inanna as a kind of liturgy, and argues that the proclamation of Inanna's divine attributes (me's) in the framework of this liturgy constitutes the veritable transfer of these attributes, and with them of supremacy among the gods, from Nanna to Inanna. It does so while recounting the fate of Enheduanna, paralleling that of Inanna, in almost autobiographical terms.

Thus the literary evidence constitutes a sizable and consistent body of work. The temple hymn shows us Enheduanna as a kind of systematic theologian, well versed in the subtleties of a—perhaps already traditional—set of Sumerian beliefs, and capable of adapting them to a new point of view (see below). The cycle of hymns to Inanna, on the other hand, reveals a less objective but at the same time more passionately involved author, striving to plead the cause of her goddess in terms that bring her ever closer to her audience: beginning with Inanna's triumphs among the barbarians of Mt. Ebih, describing her role among civilized men in general, and ending with her cultic primacy in Ur and Uruk, ancient centers of Sumerian religion.

Note what appears like a somewhat similar progression in "Inanna and Sukalletuda." After traversing Elam and Subir,[25] Inanna plagues Sumer[26] and, when that fails to achieve her purpose, proceeds to Eridu as the text breaks off.[27] In other respects, too, this composition seems to be dependent on the great cycle of hymns to Inanna.[28] Indeed, just as Enheduanna's combination of princely and priestly roles was precedent-making (barring the discovery of still earlier antecedents), so too her poetic efforts must have served as a model for much subsequent hymnography. It may remain for literary criticism to trace the influence of her writings on other and later compositions;[29] here we can only stress, as a likely index of such influence, the unusual popularity her poems enjoyed in the Old Babylonian period. The poem nin-me-šár-ra which is offered herewith is not only listed in several literary catalogues of that period,[30] but the relatively brief text of 153 lines is attested by, and reconstructed below from, nearly fifty different exemplars. This is twice as many as, for example, the familiar and popular hymn to Enlil called ^{d}en-líl sù-rá-šè[31] or the best attested hymns to the kings of Ur[32]

25. Kramer, *ArOr 17/1* (1949), 401, n. 13.
26. The kalam; ibid., p. 404.
27. Ibid., pp. 403 f.
28. Cf. below, note 46, and notes 19 and 60 to Chapter 5.
29. For some possible examples, see below, pp. 5 f.
30. See below, Chapter 3, notes 10 and 11.
31. Ed. by Falkenstein, *SGL, 1* (1959), No. 1.
32. Šulgi A, ed. by Falkenstein, *ZA, 50* (1952), 63–91.

and Isin,[33] though admittedly the publication of duplicates not utilized in their editions would tend to redress the imbalance.[34]

A most telling symptom of the place Enheduanna attained for herself in the eyes of her countrymen was her virtual apotheosis in the later theology. We find her name, albeit without the divine determinative, in a late hymn to Dumuzi in the midst of a long succession of epithets of the god.[35] It may be that it, too, is here an epithet of Dumuzi, like en-nun-gal-an-na, en-sipa-zi-an-na, ù-mu-un-du$_6$-šub$^!$-ba-ke$_4$, ù-mu-un-a-ra-li-ke$_4$ etc. But even then it could perhaps be interpreted as "(the one whose) en is Heduanna," for we also meet Heduanna—as a manifestation of the moongod Sin in the (late) canonical god-lists.[36] Although one cannot simply equate the divine name with that of the priestess, it nonetheless seems possible, therefore, that en in the fuller form is virtually a title, for other instances of its omission could be cited.[37] In our own poem, she emerges at the end (l. 149) as an embodiment of Ningal who, as consort of the moongod, also claimed her services (l. 119). But above all, she appears as a kind of Inanna, the goddess to whom she was personally devoted. For in the, in part post-Sumerian, "Inanna laments," that deity's exile from her temples is described in a manner wholly reminiscent of Enheduanna's removal from the priesthood in nin-me-šár-ra. A few examples will have to suffice.

In line 98 of our poem, there is an obscure reference to "beaching your ship of mourning on a hostile shore." With this may be compared the picture of Inanna fleeing by boat in her laments.[38] In line 105, Enheduanna compares herself to a swallow fleeing its coop; just so Inanna complains that she is made to fly out of her "house" (temple) like a bird.[39] As Enheduanna wears the crown appropriate to the office of high-priestess (l. 107 and above, p. 2), so Inanna is suited for the same office and enamored of its appropriate crown (l. 4). As Enheduanna was stripped of the tiara (l. 107), so Inanna is stripped of her garment and jewels by the "enemy,"[40] who clothed his own wife and daughters with them.[41]

---

33. Lipit-Ištar *23, ed. by W. H. Ph. Römer, *SKIZ*, 29–38.

34. Miss Gertrud Flügge, for example, has utilized 45 examplars for her unpublished edition of Lipit-Ištar* 23. Lexical texts and proverbs, since they formed the basis of all instruction, are of course even more plentifully attested. Cf. also E. I. Gordon, *Sumerian Proverbs* (1959), pp. 19 f.

35. *CT* 42:15 i 20; cf. the review by S. N. Kramer, *JCS*, *18* (1964), 45, n. 76.

36. *CT* 25:42:7; cf. A. Deimel, *Pantheon Babylonicum* (1914), No. 461.

37. Cf. Edzard, *ZA*, *53* (1959), 9–26, esp. 15 ff.

38. Cf. Falkenstein, *SAHG* No. 33:12–15; St. Langdon, *Babylonian Liturgies* (1913), 71:25 f.

39. *SAHG* No. 33:29; *BL* 71:40.

40. *SAHG* No. 33:21 f.; *BL* 71:32 f.

41. Ibid.

One of the most striking coincidences in the language of the two genres is represented by the expression "Fluttering like bats they fly off from before you to the clefts (of the rock)." In our poem (l. 35), as in an early Ur III incantation from Drehem,[42] this topos is applied to the Anunna; in the laments it is applied to Inanna herself,[43] but the wording is virtually identical. Thus Enheduanna appears to be confused, if not precisely identified, with one or another of the deities whom she served, particularly Inanna. This raises some significant historical questions.

In the first place it is legitimate to ask whether this confusion, not to say identification, was really only a late development, or whether in fact our customary definitions of deity and deification are not a little too circumscribed when applied to the third millennium. We are familiar, notably from Catholic usage, with the notion of canonization, of the elevation of a deceased human being to a rank worthy of worship or at least devotion, in recognition of outstanding achievements or exemplary conduct during his or her lifetime. It seems at least conceivable that Enheduanna, together with many other historical figures such as, for example, Gudea, Ur-Nammu, and Zariqum, enjoyed a similar posthumous treatment.

But we can go further and suggest that the constantly changing status of the different gods in Mesopotamian theogony and theology may have at times reflected the actual fortunes of their priestly counterparts on earth. Thus the elevation of Inanna-Ištar, which plays such a pervasive role in both Sumerian and Akkadian theology, may well have originated with Sargon of Akkad. According to one legend, the Akkadian usurper was himself the illicit(?) product of a union between a high priestess and an unknown father.[44] In the King List tradition, this father(?) was a "gardener," an epithet apparently applied to kings or their substitutes in the "sacred marriage" of the New Years' ritual,[45] but reminiscent here also of Inanna's seduction by the gardener Sukkaletuda in the Sumerian tradition and of her seduction of Išullanu the gardener in the Akkadian Gilgameš epic.[46] It may further be supposed that Sargon's rise to prominence at the Sumerian court of Kiš was in alliance with a Sumerian priestess representing the Sumerian goddess, for, as the aforementioned legend puts it, he won "Ištar's" love as a youth and in the guise of a gardener. Thus the exaltation of the goddess would be reflected by a historical tradition which makes Sargon variously the son, lover, or father

42. H. de Genouillac, *La Trouvaille de Dréhem* (1911), 1:4, 11; cf. most recently Falkenstein, *AS, 16* (1965), 136(g).
43. *SAHG* No. 33:28; *BL* 71:39.
44. *CT* 13:42:1–4; cf. *CAD,E*, 173a.
45. Cf. Weisbach, *RLA, 1* (1938), 390 f. s.v. Enlilbâni.
46. Cf. Kramer, *ArOr 17/1* (1949), 400–02; Speiser, *ANET*, p. 84.

of a priestess representing the goddess, and the three great hymns of Enheduanna dedicated to Inanna would then represent a major contribution by Sargon's brilliant daughter to the propagation of the new theology.

In the second place there is, historically, no question but that Enheduanna stood in the service of the moongod Nanna of Ur. How, then, are we to explain her near-identification with Inanna, and indeed the outspoken pro-Inanna bias of her poetry? Our poem may be said to provide an answer quite consonant with the historical situation in the early Old Akkadian period as we know it at present from other sources.

When Sargon began his struggle for the hegemony of "Sumer and Akkad," Mesopotamian constitutional organization was based on a system of largely independent city-states united in a loose and primarily cultic league. Among these cities, however, three had long monopolized, by turns, such hegemony as the league was willing to acknowledge. These were Kiš in the north and Ur and Uruk in the south.[47] Moreover, Ur and Uruk had already then a tradition of dynastic union which meant that they more often than not acted in concert. Sargon first rose to prominence at the court of Kiš; it was in this area that he founded his own new city-state of Akkad; and it was as king of Kiš that he laid claim to a greater dominion. His principal opponent was Lugalzagesi who, starting from an equally modest base in Umma, won the hegemony of Sumer by successfully laying claim to the kingship of Uruk and Ur. When, therefore, Sargon defeated Lugalzagesi, the condominium of Ur and Uruk fell to him by right of conquest. He assumed those titles and functions of Lugalzagesi which stressed this claim, and he strengthened it by a new and cultically critical institution: the installation of his daughter as high priestess and "bride" of the moongod at Ur and—we must suppose—of his "sister" as priestess and bride of the Heaven-god at Uruk. Such, at any rate, is the literal implication of the title pa_4-šeš-an-(na) which he was the first to assume.[48] This title, which reflected his rule over Uruk,[49] meant not "anointing anointed priest of An" as formerly translated[50] but rather "older brother, brother-in-

47. Cf. F. R. Kraus, *ZA, 50* (1952), 55–57, for the reflection of this historical reality in the King-List tradition.

48. According to *CAD,A,*/1:204d, he was followed in this usage by his son Maništušu. The reference is to the fragmentary first column of his Cruciform Monument which, though the rest of the document was largely an Old Babylonian forgery, may in this instance have been copied from authentic originals; cf. Gelb, *JNES, 8* (1949), 348, n. 11. Note that the title is fully preserved in the neo-Babylonian copy published by Thureau-Dangin, *RA,* 7 (1910), 180, where, however, it is written PA.ŠEŠ AN.

49. Hallo, *Early Mesopotamian Royal Titles* (1957), pp. 5 f.; for older interpretations, cf. Hirsch, *AfO, 20* (1963), 78 f.

50. See references in *CAD,A,*/1:205a s.v. *ahu rabû = rabi ahi,* where this translation is rejected.

law of An." In this sense it is generally confined to gods,[51] but the usage here is no more startling than the Middle Babylonian usage "father-in-law of Nanna" to designate Adad-apal-iddina as the king whose daughter served as high priestess-and-bride of the moongod at Ur.[52] As Edzard has shown, however, the Sumerian kinship terminology is a functional rather than a strictly genealogical one:[53] the term "brother-in-law" could readily come to stand for the older male person who was guardian of one's bride before her marriage, whether as brother or father. It is thus a fairly moot point whether Sargon's in-law relationship to An was based originally on a sister or a daughter; certainly Enheduanna seems, eventually if not at once, to have served also at Uruk. In the latter function, Enheduanna must have been regarded as the virtual personification of Inanna who, by the same token, was elevated to equal rank with An. [But see Addenda 1.]

There is, indeed, indirect evidence from a more recent period to a dual residence, if not office, of high priestess of Nanna. For in addition to her *gipāru* at Ur, there was another at Karzida which, after long neglect, Amar-Sin built or rebuilt for the high priestess of Nanna of Karzida. According to Sollberger,[54] this lady was distinct from the contemporary high priestess of Nanna at Ur, although he admits that the latter's predecessor may also have resided at Karzida.[55] But whether in separate persons or in one person under different names, it is clear that the high priestess of Nanna functioned at the *gipāru* of Karzida as well as at that of Ur in the Ur III period.[56]

We do not, as at Ur, possess contemporary inscriptions from Uruk attesting to Enheduanna's presence and functioning there. But her very name was, like the names of all but one of her successors, compounded with An. It was, of

51. E.g. Ninurta in *BE* 29/1:1 ii 34 and *STVC* 35:72 f.; cf. Falkenstein, *SGL* 1:119.

52. *UET* 1:166 f.; cf. B. Landsberger, *OLZ* (1931), c. 129.

53. *CRRAI, 9* (1960) (= *Genava* 8, 1960), 253–57.

54. *AfO, 17* (1954–56), 28 f.

55. Ibid., pp. 19 and 28 f.

56. This particular kar-zi-da (literally, "good quay") was situated at Gaeš, a port city (cf. the loan word *k/gaiššu* = merchant), for whose location cf. Oppenheim, *JAOS, 74* (1954), 4, n. 22: "quite near to Ur if it was not actually a suburb or quarter of this very town," and Falkenstein, Friedrich *AV* (1959): probably "nicht weit von Ur entfernt gelegen." It should be noted, however, that all the relevant building inscriptions (Amar-Sin 6, 8, and 11 in my bibliography, *HUCA, 33* [1963], 35 f. and 43) are of unknown provenience except the last, and both exemplars of this (*UVB, 10* [1939], 18 f.; *UVB, 12/13* [1956], 25) come from Uruk! Although it is true that these two pivot stones were reused by Merodach-baladan II in the building of the temple of Ningizzida (cf. R. North, *Or., 26* [1957], 223 f.), one wonders how far they may have been brought from their original site, and it has even been suggested that they may have come from a "temple" built by Amar-Sin in the "lower court" of Eanna at Uruk itself (H. Lenzen, *Iraq, 19* [1957], 149 f.; *22* [1960], 132, 134).

course, a cult name, carefully chosen, it would seem, to suggest both her priestly role and her ties to Uruk. For it is attested in an early literary text as a priestly name at Lagaš[57] and in the Sumerian King List as a princely name at pre-Sargonic Uruk.[58] As for the princess' dual cultic role at Ur and Uruk, this would parallel the aforementioned dual political role of her father. Her poem supports this conclusion. For although neither Ur nor Uruk are mentioned in it by name, the divine protagonists are, apart from Inanna, precisely the deities of those two cities, the moongod and the god of Heaven respectively. Enheduanna is expelled from both places, that is from both her priestly roles, and pleads in vain with both Nanna and An for the restoration which, in the end, she owes to Inanna.

The historical tradition amply confirms the uneasy peace which the Sargonic kings imposed on both Ur and Uruk. In Ur, for example, we know of a rival king, Kaku, as late as the reign of Rimuš, from the Nippur copies of the Sargonic royal inscriptions. At Uruk, we know from "legendary texts"[59] that a certain Lugalanne or Lugalanna played a role in the great revolt against Naram-Sin, and it seems difficult to dissociate these later traditions from the Lugalanne whose role in the present hymn is painted in such negative terms. It seems, then, entirely possible that Sargon, in a conscious effort to replace the loose alliance of Sumer and Akkad with a truly centralized imperial system, adapted the existing cultic and dynastic institutions of the south to his own purposes—that he not only perpetuated the dynastic union of Ur and Uruk in his own person, but instituted a cultic union of their chief priestly offices in the person of his daughter Enheduanna, the devotee of Inanna. We may even see in this assumed state of affairs a partial explanation of the Sargonic break with the well-attested tradition of expressing the condominium of Ur and Uruk as a kingship of Ur and en-ship of Uruk.[60]

As a final step in this politico-religious reformation, Sargon equated the Sumerian Inanna with the Akkadian Ištar to lay the theological foundations for a united empire of Sumer and Akkad, and thus ushered in what the

---

57. Written en-hé-du₁₀-an-na; *NFT* 2:202 obv. ii 3; cf. Falkenstein, *RA, 52* (1958), 129, n. 7.

58. Reading en-hé!!- du-an-na in WB iv 45, *contra* Jacobsen, *SKL*, p. 171, and restoring the same in Ni 9217b v 1 for which cf. the copy by Kramer, *UMB* 17:19 and the remarks by Kraus, *ZA, 50* (1952), 36.

59. A Boissier, *RA, 16* (1919), 163, l. 42; cf. Güterbock, *ZA, 42* (1934), 77 (Old Babylonian; written Lugal-an-na); Gelb, *Hurrians and Subarians* (1944), p. 56, n. 56 = *MAD, 1* (1952), 172 (Old Akkadian; written Lugal-an-né).

60. Hallo, *Titles*, pp. 3–8; perhaps Sargon and Naram-Sin felt that the religious claims of their daughters were less offensive to Sumerian sensibilities than their own political pretensions. Cf. now also Sollberger, *UET* 8:12 and p. 3, for an Akkadian inscription of Naram-Sin's priestly daughter from Ur.

chronographic tradition regarded as the "dynasty of Ishtar."[61] The notion
that a rival designation of the Sargonic period as the "age of Nanna" (a-di-i
ᵈnannari) was current in the neo-Assyrian period,[62] improbable enough in
the light of "Sargonic theology" generally and nin-me-šár-ra in particular, is based on a misreading of the passages in question, which should
rather be understood as "from distant days until now" (a-di i-nanna).[63]
Enheduanna's cycle of temple hymns to Inanna[64] could well have celebrated
this reformation for, as Falkenstein has seen,[65] it is unique in linking the
temples and cult centers of Akkad with those of Sumer. In sum, it seems that
the role of Inanna-Ištar is equally prominent in the Sumerian as in the later
Akkadian "historical tradition" concerning Sargon, and that it rests on an
authentic historical basis of its own, rather than on a kind of "Eannatum-
typology" as has recently been suggested.[66]

One further question deserves to be aired in this connection, and this is
our poem's puzzling reluctance to refer to Inanna by name. It is striking that,
in all its 153 lines, this paean of uninterrupted praise to the goddess manages
to invoke her name only four times. And not once does Enheduanna directly
address the goddess as Inanna, not even in the place where Sumerian hymns
to gods otherwise do so as a matter of course, that is at the beginning of the
second line or strophe in parallelism to the opening epithet. Instead, line 3
invokes the deity by another epithet which, while most often applied to
Inanna, is also employed of other goddesses.[67]

The actual mentions of Inanna are all qualified in one way or another. In
the first (l. 12), Enheduanna merely states that her goddess is literally, "of
heaven and earth—their Inanna." Although this expression is not entirely
unparalleled,[68] it means little more than "you are their goddess," and it
hardly compensates for the direct invocation of the divine name called for
well before this in the poem.

The second mention of Inanna's name (l. 83) occurs, precisely, in the one
stanza of Enheduanna's long speech which is definitely *not* addressed to the

61. King, *Chronicles Concerning Early Babylonian Kings*, 2:3:1; 2:31:23. Cf.
Jacobsen, *JNES, 2* (1943), 170 and n. 67.

62. J. Lewy, *HUCA, 19* (1946), 443, 461–89, who drew a number of far-reaching
conclusions largely on this basis.

63. For similar spellings elsewhere, cf. *CAD,I*, 143d. For the meaning of adû
(=á-dù-a) in the "Exaltation of Ištar" (*RA, 11* [1914], 156 = *TCL* 6:51, l. 28),
cf. *CAD,A,*/1 135 bc.

64. See above, n. 19.

65. *RA, 52* (1958), 129 and n. 6.

66. H. Hirsch, "Eannatum von Lagaš und Sargon von Agade," *Studies Presented
to A. Leo Oppenheim* (1964), pp. 136–39. Cf. the review by K. Riemschneider, *ArOr,
34* (1966), 428 f.

67. Below, Chapter 5, note 7.

68. Cf. Glossary s.v. ᵈinanna.

goddess. And even in this stanza, Inanna is, on our interpretation, twice referred to as "this [respectively, that] woman" with what appears to be intentional obscurity. The third mention (l. 145) occurs outside of Enheduanna's speech altogether, in what is probably a kind of stereotyped denouement if not actually a secondary editorial addition to the original composition. The last is in the standard closing formula of the entire poem (l. 153).

Ordinarily, the Sumerian poets certainly had no scruples, religious or stylistic, about addressing the deity by name. Enheduanna's reticence in this respect seems the more remarkable as she found more than forty different epithets, apart from numerous similes and other descriptions, wherewith to address the goddess while avoiding, as it seems, her name. Nor is the same reticence characteristic of the other compositions for Inanna attributed, or attributable, to Enheduanna. To regard it as coincidental in the present context seems therefore as difficult as it is to find a convincing reason for it. But perhaps the aforementioned aim to achieve a syncretism between Inanna and Ištar had some bearing on the question.[69]

With this brief appreciation of its historical and literary setting, we can now proceed to a presentation of the hymn itself, first in transliteration and translation. This will be followed by a slightly more detailed analysis not, however, in the form of the usual line-by-line commentary, but treating separately and in succession the textual, structural, contextual, and lexical problems raised by our text.

69. A similar problem seems to have exercised Enheduanna's successor, Enmenanna. According to her new inscription (cf. above, n. 60), this daughter of Naram-Sin styled herself "spouse of Nanna, high priestess of Suen." It is not clear whether this phraseology was intended to emphasize the distinctiveness or the identity of the two divine names.

nin-me-šár-ra: Transliteration and Translation

The following transliteration employs the Sumerian values as given by Labat, *Manuel d'epigraphie accadienne* (1948). It is based on A + X, photographs of which appear as Plates 1–3. This text was collated from the original, and collations are indicated by asterisks. Where the text was broken or, in our opinion, defective, restorations (marked ˙ ˙) and emendations (marked +) were supplied from the duplicates, as indicated in the critical apparatus. For the sigla of all the exemplars, see below, pages 36 f. For many of the ideas and idioms as reflected in our translation, see Chapters 4 and 5, respectively, below.

[Upper edge]   DIŠ ^{d}nisaba nin-dub-mà-a

(i)

[i] 1 nin-me-^{a}šár-$^+$ra^a u$_4^b$-dalla-è-a
     2 ·mí·-zi me-lám gùr-ru   ki-ága-an-uraš-a^a

     3 nu-gig-an-na   *suh-kešda^a-gal-gal-la
     4 aga-zi-dè ki-ága   nam-en-na túm-ma

     5 me-imin-bé   šu sá-du$_{11}$-ga
     6 nin-mu me-gal-gal-la^a sag-kešda-bi za-e-me-en

     7 me mu-^{a}íl   me šu-zu-šè^b mu-e-lá

     8 me mu-^{a}ur$_4$ me gaba-zu^b bí^c-tab

(ii)

     9 ušumgal-gim kur-ra^a uš$_x$(KA × SU)^b ^{c}ba-e^c-sì
    10 ^{d}iškur-gim^a ki-sig$_x$(KA × LI)^b- ^{d}ezinu la-ba^e-ši-gál^f
        gi$_4^c$-*za^d

    11 a-ma-ru kur-bi-ta   e$_{11}^a$-dè
    12 sag-kal an-ki-a ^{d}inanna-bi-me-en

Upper edge: A only; for a similar notation, cf. Hallo, *Bi. Or. 23* (1966), 243.

1 $^{a-a}$Emended from colophons, catalogues, and all other exemplars; A: du$_{10}$-ga;
   ^{b}N: u$_4$-BAR-.
2 ^{a}N: -e.
3 ^{a}U$_2$: -kešd-re.
6 ^{a}N and e omit.
7 ^{a}B, N, U$_2$, a, d, and e insert -e-; ^{b}N: -uš.
8 ^{a}B, N, U$_2$, Z, a, d, and e insert -e-; ^{b}N, R, e, g, and n: -za; U$_2$: -zu-šè; ^{c}N, R,
   (and U$_2$?): ba-e-.

A. EXORDIUM

(i) Inanna and the me's

1	Lady of all the me's,	resplendent light,
2	Righteous woman clothed in radiance,	beloved of Heaven and Earth,
3	Hierodule of An	(you) of all the great ornaments,
4	Enamored of the appropriate tiara,	suitable for the high priest-hood
5	Whose hand has attained	(all) the "seven" me's,
6	Oh my lady, you are the guardian	of all the great me's!
7	You have picked up the me's,	you have hung the me's on your hand,
8	You have gathered up the me's,	you have clasped the me's to your breast.

(ii) Inanna and An

9 Like a dragon you have deposited venom on the land

10 When you roar at the earth like Thunder, no vegetation can stand up to you.

11 A flood descending from its mountain,

12 Oh foremost one, you are the Inanna of heaven and earth!

---

9 ᵃT: [ki-bal]a-ke₄ or [GAL.UŠU]M-ke₄; a, g, n, and r: -re; ᵇN, R, and T: uš₉ (KA × úš); ᶜ⁻ᶜR: bí-sí.

10 ᵃN inserts 10-line mark (U); ᵇN: KA × ?; ᶜN and l: -gi-; ᵈall other texts: -a-za; ᵉR, r, and u insert -e-; ᶠN: gub; T: gar.

11 ᵃè?-.

13   izi-ne-ne-ra   kalam-*e [a]šèg-gá
14   an-né[a] me-sì-[+]ma[b]   nin ur-ra[c] u_5-a

15   inim-kù-an-na[a]-ta   inim-du_{11}-du_{11}
16   billuda[a]-gal-gal[b]-la[c]   nì-zu a-ba[d] mu-un[e]-zu

(iii)

17   kur-gul-gul u_4-dè[a] á ba-e-sì
18   ki-ága [d]en-líl-lá   kalam-ma[a] im[b]-mi-ni[c]-dal

19   á-ága[a]-*an(a)[b]-ke_4[c]   ba-gub-bé-*[d]en
20   [a]nin-mu za-pa-*ág-zu-šè   kur[b] [c]ì-gurum-gurum-e[c]

21   ní-me-lám *u_x-*lu-da[a]   nam-lú-[b]u_x-*lu[b]
22   nì-me[a]-gar[b]-huš-bi   [cd]ù-mu-re[e]-gin[d]
23   me-*ta[a] me-huš-bi   šu [b]ba-e[c]-re-ti[b]

24   i-lu[a]-ír-ra-*ke_4[b]-gál   *ma[c]-ra-ab[d]-$še_8$[e]
25   é-a-nir[a]-gal-gal-la[b]   sila-ba mu-re[c]-gin[d]

(iv)

26   igi[a]-mè-ta   nì ma-ra-ta[b]-si-ig
27   nin-mu á-ní-za[a]   KA.KA ì-$durud_x$(KÚ)-e[b]

---

13   [a]N inserts im-.
14   [a]e wrongly: -usan; [b]A (and r?): -gá; [c]e: -a.
15   [a]W omits.
16   [a]l: [bil]luda ([PA].AN)[da]-; [b]U_2 omits; [c]C, e, g, and r omit; [d]e, g, r, and s add -a;
      [e]N insert -≪mu-un≫-.
17   [a]N: -da.
18   [a]U_2 and n: -e; [b]g: nam-; [c]N and g: -in-; U_2: -ni-in.
19   [a]All others: -ág-gá-; [b]all others: -an-na; [c]U_2 adds ≪-eš≫; [d]A: erasure (me?!).
20   [a]W inserts 10-line mark (AŠ); [b]N inserts 10-line mark (U); $U_{1,2}$ add: -≪ra≫;
      [c-c]U_2: gurun-gurun-me-en.

| 13 | Raining the fanned fire | down upon the nation, |
| 14 | Endowed with me's by An, | lady mounted on a beast, |

| 15 | Who makes decisions | at the holy command of An. |
| 16 | (You) of all the great rites, | who can fathom what is yours? |

(iii) Inanna and Enlil

| 17 | Devastatrix of the lands, | you are lent wings by the storm. |
| 18 | Beloved of Enlil, | you fly about in the nation. |

| 19 | You are at the service | of the decrees of An. |
| 20 | Oh my lady, at the sound of you | the lands bow down. |

21	When mankind	comes before you
22	In fear and trembling	at (your) tempestuous radiance,
23	They receive from you	their just deserts.

| 24 | Proffering a song of lamentation, | they weep before you, |
| 25 | They walk toward you along the path | of the house of all the great sighs. |

(iv) Inanna and Iškur

| 26 | In the van of battle | everything is struck down by you. |
| 27 | Oh my lady, (propelled) on your own wings, | you peck away (at the land). |

---

21 [a]$U_{1,2}$, U_3, and 1 omit; [b-b]so also s; all others: -ulu$_x$.

22 [a]e: -me-≪LÁM≫-; [b]N: -ME-; [c]N inserts igi-šè; [d-d]W: [igi-š] è ì-re-[gin]? [e]C: -e-re.

23 [a]A: te; all others: -ta?; [b-b]W: ì-[re-ti]?; [c]$U_{1,2}$ and U_3 omit.

24 [a]C, U_3, j, and 1: -la; [b]A: -zu; [c]so with most texts; A, W, (and CH?): la-; g: ma?-a?; [d]U_2: -an-; u omits; j: -ba?; [e]j: -x.

25 [a]$U_{1,2}$: -nir-ra; [b]C, U_3, e, and s omit; [c]$U_{1,2}$: -ri-in-; [d]U_2: -du$_{11}$.

26 [a]U_3: giš-; [b]U_3 and s: -ab-ta; N, e, and n: -an-ta; j: -ab-.

27 [a]$U_{1,2}$: -zu; J: -ta; N and $U_{1,2}$ add -dúb; [b]u adds -en.

28	u₄-du₇-du₇-gimᵃ	ì-du₇-du₇-dèᵇ
29	u₄ gù-ra-*raᵃ-taᵇ	⁴gùᶜ im-daᵈ-abᵉ-ra-raᶠ
30	ᵈiškur-daᵃ	sigₓ(KA × LI)ᵇ mu-daᶜ-anᵈ-ᵉgi₄-gi₄ᵉ-inᶠ
31	im-hul im-hul-da	imᵃ-daᵇ-kúš-ᶜù-dèᵈ
32	gìri-zaᵃ *nu-kúš-ùᵇ	ᶜi-inᶜ-si
33	balag-ᵃa-nirᵃ-⁺raᵇ-daᶜ	i-lu ᵈmu-unᵈ-ᵉda-abᵉ-béᶠ

(v)

34	nin-mu ᵈa-nun-na	dingir-gal-gal-e-ne
35	su-din mušenᵃ-dal-aᵇ-gim	du₆ᶜ-dèᵈ mu-eᵉ-šiᶠ-baᵍ-ra-ašʰ
36	igi-huš-a-*zaᵃ	la-baᵇ-su₈ᶜ-ge-ᵈeš-aᵈ
37	sag-ki-huš-a-zaᵃ	sag nu-mu-unᵇ-dèᶜ-gá-gá
38	šà-íb-baᵃ-zaᵇ	a-baᶜ ìᵈ-te-enᵉ-te-en
39	šà-hul-gál-laᵃ-zaᵇ	te-enᶜ-teᵈ-bi mah-aᵉ
40	nin ur₅ᵃ ì-ša₆ᵇ	nin šà ì-húlᶜ
41	íb-ba nu-te-en-te-en	dumu-gal-ᵈsu'enᵃ-naᵇ
42	nin kurᵃ-ra diri-ga	a-ba ki-zaᵇ ba-an-tùmᶜ

---

28 ᵃN (and C, W, n?): -da; e (and g?): -dè; ᵇH, N, U₁, U₃¹, g, l, s, and u: -dè-en; U₂: -da; j: -gim.
29 ᵃU₁,₂ omit; ᵇN, U₁,₂, e, g, j, n, s, and u: -da; ᶜA: UN; U₃: kú; ᵈr: x-y; ᵉs omits; ᶠu adds: -an.
30 ᵃU₃: -gim; N inserts 10-line mark (U); ᵇKA × ?; ᶜN, U₁,₂, and s: -un-da-; ᵈU₁,₂ and U₃: -ab-; N and u: omit; ᵉ⁻ᵉN: -gi-gi; ᶠso also N and u; others omit.
31 ᵃQ: in-; ᵇN inserts -an-; ᶜN: -kùš-≪kùš≫-; ᵈH, N, s, and u: -dè-en; U₂: -di-en.
32 ᵃU₁, l, and n: -zu; ᵇQ: -e; ᶜ⁻ᶜU₁, U₃, and n: i-im-; N, Q, j, and l: im-.
33 ᵃ⁻ᵃU₃: -ír-; ᵇA omits; ᶜN, Q, U₁, U₃, e, and l: -ta; j omits; ᵈ⁻ᵈN, U₁, U₃, W, q, (and n?): -im-; H: [im]-mi-; ᵉ⁻ᵉH and Q: -dab-; ᶠs adds -en.
35 ᵃn omits; ᵇN: -la-; S and e omit; ᶜN: du₁₀-; ᵈQ: -da; S: -du₇; ᵉe: -un-; U₃ omits; ᶠS: -šè?-; ᵍor ib?; N, e, l, q, (and n?): ib; G, Q, and U₃: -íb-; ʰl and s: -áš?

28	In the guise of a charging storm	you charge.
29	With a roaring storm	you roar.
30	With Thunder	you continually thunder.
31	With all the evil winds	you snort.
32	Your feet are filled	with restlessness.
33	To (the accompaniment of) the harp of sighs	you give vent to a dirge.

(v) Inanna and the Anunna

34	Oh my lady, the Anunna,	the great gods,
35	Fluttering like bats	fly off from before you to the clefts,
36	They who dare not walk(?)	in your terrible glance,
37	Who dare not proceed	before your terrible countenance.
38	Who can temper	your raging heart?
39	Your malevolent heart	is beyond tempering.
40	Lady (who) soothes the reins,	lady (who) gladdens the heart,
41	Whose rage is not tempered,	oh eldest daughter of Suen!
42	Lady supreme over the land,	who has (ever) denied (you) homage?

36 ᵃS and U_1: -zu; ᵇj inserts -ab-; ᶜU_3: -sì-; ᵈ⁻ᵈso also e (and G ?); N, U_3, q, (and U_1, j ?): -dè-eš; Q (and n ?): -eš-àm.

37 ᵃS and U_1: -zu; ᵇU_3 and e omit; ᶜQ (and S ?): -di-.

38 ᵃU_1, U_3, and j insert -a-; ᵇS, U_1, (and n ?): -zu; ᶜN, S, and n add -a; U_1 adds -àm; ᵈN, Q, e, n, and q: íb-; S: mu-un; ᵉj omits.

39 ᵃU_1 inserts -a-; ᵇS, U_1, n, (and Z ?): -zu; ᶜU_1: -íb-; ᵈN and e insert -en-; ᵉG: -am₆; N, Q, S, U_1, and e: -àm.

40 ᵃS: šà; ᵇN inserts 10-line mark (U); ᶜN: -ša₆.

41 ᵃS: zu.ᵈEN?; ᵇN omits.

42 ᵃN: šár-?; S: an-; ᵇS: -zu?; ᶜso also N; Q, S, and U_2: túm.

(vi)

43   hur^a-sag ki-za ^{b}ba-‘e-dè-sù‘-dè^b ^{d}ezinu nì-gig-bi

44   ká-gal-a^a-b·é^b d·è mu-^{c}ni-in^c-dal^d

[ii] 45   *i$_7$^{a}-ba^b úš ·ma-ra-an^c-dé^d ùku-bé^e +ba^f-ra-nag^g-nag·

46   ugnim^a-·bi   ní-bi-a^b ma-ra-ab-lah$_4$(DU + DU)^c-e^d·

47   ka-kešda-b·i   ní-bi-a^a ma-ra-ab^b-si-il-e·^{c}

48   guruš-^{a}á-tuku^a-bi   ní-bi-a   ma-·ra-ab^b-^{c}su$_8$-ge^c-eš·^{d}

49   uru^a-ba ki-+e^b-ne^c-*di^d-bé^e mir^f ^{g}i-in^g-si

50   guruš-^{a}šà-gan-bi^a ^{b}lú-éše^b ma-ra-ab-sar-·re-eš·

(vii)

51   uru^a kur za^b-ra^c ^{d}li-bí-in^d-du$_{11}$-ga^e

52   a-a-ugu-za^a ^{b}li-bí^c-in^b-eš^d-*a^e

53   inim-kù-zu^a bí^b-in^c-du$_{11}$^{d} ka^e-gìri-za^f hé-eb^g-gi$_4$^{h}

54   šà-tùr-bi-ta   gìri hé^a-éb^b-ta^c-an-zé^d-*er

55   mí-bé dam-a-ni-ta^a ša$_6$-ga^b ^{c}na-+an^c-da-ab-bé

56   gi$_6$^{a}-ù-na   ad ^{b}na-an^b-*^{c}di-ni-ib^c-^{d}gi$_4$-gi$_4$^{d}

57   nì-kù-šà-ga-na^a nam-mu-da-an^b-búr-re^c

43 ^{a}S: kur-; $^{b-b}$restored from U$_2$; N adds: -en; Q: bad-rá-dè; S: bi-LU-sù-da. A: ba-[. . .]-dè; n: ba-e-da-sù-da.

44 ^{a}N, Q, S, and U$_2$: -la-; ^{b}E, F, N, k, and n: -ba; $^{c-c}$N and U$_2$: -e-; S: -un-; Q omits; ^{d}N, Q, and U$_2$: -dal-dal; S: sì.

45 Restored from N. ^{a}S: a-ambar-; ^{b}S: -bi; ^{c}U$_2$ omits; ^{d}U$_2$: tùm; E adds -e; ^{e}U$_2$ (and n?): -e; ^{f}emended from U$_2$; all others: ma-; ^{g}S: -ni$^!$-; n: -ab-nag.

46 Restored from N and Q. ^{a}S: erín-; ^{b}S (and n?) omit; ^{c}U$_2$ and S: -gin-; ^{d}n: -eš.

47 Restored from N. ^{a}S and n omit; ^{b}n omits; ^{c}Q, T, U$_2$, (and E?): -le; n: -le-eš.

48 Restored from N. S omits lines 48–50; N and U$_1$ partly conflate lines 48–50. $^{a-a}$N: šà-gan (cf. line 50); ^{b}n omits; $^{c-c}$U$_1$: -sar-re- (cf. line 50); ^{d}U$_2$ omits.

49 ^{a}U$_{1,2}$: urú-; ^{b}A omits; ^{c}s omits; ^{d}N omits; ^{e}U$_{1,2}$: -di; N, W, (and s?): -ba; ^{f}U$_{1,2}$ (and W?) add -re; Q adds -e-; $^{g-g}$U$_{1,2}$: im-; W and n: ib?-; N: i-íb-; Q: ì-íb-.

50 Restored from N and Q. See above, line 48. $^{a-a}$N: á-tug (cf. line 48); $^{b-b}$U$_{1,2}$: ad(da)$_x$-šè.

(vi) Inanna and Ebih(?)

43 In the mountain where homage is withheld from you vegetation is
    accursed.

44 Its grand entrance   you have reduced to ashes.

45 Blood rises in its rivers for you, its people have nought to drink.

46 It leads its army captive before you of its own accord.

47 It disbands its regiments before you of its own accord.

48 It makes its able-bodied young men parade before you of their own
    accord.

49 A tempest has filled the dancing of its city.

50 It drives its young adults before you as captives.

(vii) Inanna and Uruk

51 Over the city which has not de-   "The land is yours,"
    clared

52 Which has not declared   "It is your father's, your begettor's"

53 You have spoken your holy com-   have verily turned it back from
    mand,   your path,

54 Have verily removed your foot   from out of its byre.

55 Its woman no longer speaks of   with her husband.
    love

56 At night they no longer   have intercourse.

57 She no longer reveals to him   her inmost treasures.

---

51 [a]$U_{1,2}$ and t: urú; S: uru^{KI}; [b]R and u insert -a-; [c]S: -e; [d-d]S: la-ba-an-; $U_{1,2}$:
    li-bi-; [e]S adds -a; Q, n, (and t?) add -àm; $U_{1,2}$ adds -me?

52 [a]D, O, R, S, $U_{1,2}$, n, and t: -zu; [b-b]S: la-ba-an-; [c]$U_{1,2}$: -bi-; [d]O: -ne-eš; Q:
    gi$_4$-eš-; S: -šE-; [e]D, Q, S, $U_{1,2}$, n, (and t?): -àm; O omits; N adds colophon:
    51 mu-bi-im.

53 [a]T, W, and u: -za; [b]R: ù-bi-; O, W, n, and u: ù-bí-; [c]W omits; [d]D: du; [e]so
    also S?; all others: ki-; [f]O, n, t, (and S, W?): -zu; D (and W?): -ba; Q: -bi?;
    [g]Q: -en-; S and t omit?; [h]D, O, (and S?): -gi.

54 [a]U_2: ha-; [b]U_2: -ab; D, E, W, n, and t: -ib-; [c]n: -da-; [d]D and O: -ze-.

55 [a]E omits; [b]E adds -ni?; [c-c]A: na-Aš-an-; D and Q: nam-.

56 [a]s: GI$_6$.A (cf. line 139); [b-b]U_2: nam-; [c-c]so also O and t: D, H, and n: -da-ab-;
    U_2: -da-?; W: -[. . .]-ni-; [d-d]E and O: -gi-gi.

57 [a]R, U_2, and W: -ni; [b]U_2 and n omit; [c]U_2 and W: -e.

58 ù-sun-zi-zi-i[a]   dumu-gal-^{d}su'en-na
59 nin an-ra diri-ga   a-ba[a] ki-za ba-an-tùm

(viii)

60 [a]me-zi-dè[b]   nin[!]-gal-nin-e-ne
61 [a]*šà-kù-ta è-a   ama-ugu-ni-ir[b] diri-ga

62 gal-zu igi-gál   nin-kur-kur-ra
63 zi-gál-ùku-lu-a   šìr[a]-kù-zu[b] ga-àm-du$_{11}$

64 dingir-zi me-a[a] túm-ma   *gal-bi-du$_{11}$-ga-$^+$zu[b] mah-a[c]
65 šà-sù[a]-rá[b] mí-zi-   me-zu[e] [f]*ga-mu-ra-ab-du$_{11}$[f]
      [c]zalzale(UD.UD)-ga[d]

(ix)

66 gi$_6$-pàr-kù-gá   hu-mu-e[a]-ši-in-ku$_4$-re[b]
67 en-me-en   *en-hé-du$_7$-an-na-[a]me-en[a]

68 ^{gi}ma-sá-ab ì-gùr-ru[a]   [b]asila^{lá} [b]ì-du$_{11}$[c]
69 ki-sì[a]-ga bí-in[b]-gar   gá-e nu-mu-un-dè[c]-[d]ti-le[d]

58 [a]So also H; D, O, R, U$_2$, W, s, t, and u omit.
59 [a]D, J, n, (and O!) add -a.
60 [a]10-line mark (U) in Q; [b]H, O, R, r, and u: -da.
61 [a]10-line mark (U) in O; [b]n omits.
63 [a]D and n omit; [b]D: -zi (cf. line 65).
64 [a]D, O, U$_2$, and o omit; [b]A and O: -bi; J: -ni; D: -a-zu[!]; [c]D: am$_6$[!].
65 [a]Q and s: -sur-; [b]U$_2$: -da; O: -ta; D: ?; Q and s: -ra; [c]H, J, O, and U$_2$ insert
    -šà-; D inserts -ki[?]-; [d]J, o, and u omit; [e]D (and U$_2$?): -zi; [f-f]D: hu-mu-un-
    na-ab-bé.

58 Impetuous wild cow,	great daughter of Suen,
59 Lady supreme over An	who has (ever) denied (you) homage?

(viii) Invocation of Inanna

60 You of the appropriate me's,	great queen of queens,
61 Issued from the holy womb,	supreme over the mother who bore you,
62 Omniscient sage,	lady of all the lands,
63 Sustenance of the multitudes,	I have verily recited your sacred song!
64 True goddess, fit for the me's,	it is exalting to acclaim you.
65 Merciful one, brilliantly righteous woman,	I have verily recited your me's for you!

B. THE ARGUMENT

(ix) The Banishment from Ur

66 Verily I had entered	my holy gipāru at your behest,
67 I, the high priestess,	I, Enheduanna!
68 I carried the ritual basket,	I intoned the acclaim.
69 (But now) I am placed in the lepers' ward,	I, even I, can no longer live with you!

---

66 aSo also u (and n ?); U₂: -un-; others omit; bD, H, (and s ?) add -en; O adds -em.
67 a-aD and O: -mu.
68 aD, O, U₂, U₄, and s omit; b-bs: asilala; D: si-il-le; cH and O: -di.
69 aD and U₂: -ša₆-; bH, i, r, s, and u: -ib-; D and J: -íb-; cJ: -di-; D, H, and O omit; d-dH and O: til-en; s: til-l[e]-.

70 u₄-dè ba-teᵃ   u₄ mu?!-daᵇ-píl
71 ᵃgizzu u₄-dèᵃ ba-teᵇ   ᶜuₓ-luᶜ-da im-miᵈ-dul

72 ka-làl-mu šu-ùh-a ba-ab-tùmᵃ
73 nì-ur₅ᵃ-ša₆-ša₆-muᵇ   *sahar-ta ba-eᶜ-dèᵈ-gi₄ᵉ

(x)

74 nam-mu ᵈ*su'enᵃ   lugal-an-*néᵇ
75 anᵃ-ra du₁₁-mu-na-abᵇ   an-eᶜ ha-ba-du₈-eᵈ

76 a-da-lam an-ra ᵃdu₁₁-mu-na-abᵃ an-eᵇ ᶜmu-eᶜ-du₈-eᵈ
77 nam-lugal-an-néᵃ   mí-e ba-ab-karᵇ-⁺reᶜ

78 kur-a-ma-ru   gìri-ni-šè ì-náᵃ
79 mí-bi inᵃ-gaᵇ-mah   uruᶜ ᵈ*mu-*taᵈ-abᵉ-tag₄ᶠ-eᵍ
80 gub-ba-šà-ga-naᵃ   ha-ma-še₈-dèᵇ

81 en-hé-du₇-an-na-ᵃme-enᵃ   a-ra-zu ga-mu-⁺raᵇ-ab-du₁₁ᶜ
82 ír-gá   kaš-du₁₀-ga-⁺gimᵃ
83 kù-ᵈinanna-ra šu gaᵃ-mu-unᵇ-reᶜ-barᵈ silim-maᵉ ga-mu-⁺naᶠ-
   ab-du₁₁ᵍ

(xi)

84 aš-ᵈ·ím·ᵃ-⁺babbarᵇ   ᶜ⁺na-an⁺ᶜ-kúš-ù-dèᵈ
85 šu-luhᵃ-an-kù-ga-ke₄ᵇ nì-namᶜ-ma-niᵈ inᵉ-kúr

---

70 ᵃD adds -en; ᵇU₂: -um-da-.
71 ᵃ⁻ᵃSo also D; J, O, n, and u: gizzu-dè; H, q, s, (and i): gizzu-e; ᵇD adds -en-na;
    ᶜ⁻ᶜD, H, and J: ulù-; ᵈO: -ma-an; s: ma?.
72 ᵃSo also s?; D, J, and O: -du₁₁; U₁: -dé?.
73 ᵃO (and U₃?): -ga; ᵇH and s: -mà; ᶜD, H, O, and U₁ omit; ᵈ all others: -da-;
    ᵉU₁: -ab-gi₄; O: -gi; D: -gi-en.
74 ᵃSo U₁; A, H, J, i, s, and u omit; D and O: -na; ᵇU₁: -na.
75 ᵃU₃: lú-; ᵇD adds: -bé; ᶜD, O, and U₁: -né; ᵈD and H: -en.
76 ᵃ⁻ᵃSo also U₄; H and O: ba-an-na-ab-bé-en; U₁: ba-an-na-ab-bé; D: ba-na-
    ab-bé; J: ba-an-na-ab-du₁₁; ᵇD, O, and U₁: an-né; ᶜ⁻ᶜD: me-; H: me-e-;
    O: mu-un-; ᵈH: e-en; D and U₁: -en.
77 ᵃU₁: -e; ᵇO: -TE-; ᶜA and D add -en.
78 ᵃU₄ adds -a?

70 They approach the light of day,   the light is obscured about me,
71 The shadows approach the light   it is covered with a (sand)storm.
        of day,

72 My mellifluous mouth is cast into confusion.
73 My choicest features   are turned to dust.

(x) The Appeal to Nanna-Suen

74 What is he to me, oh Suen,   this Lugalanne!
75 Say thus to An: "May An release me!"

76 Say but to An "Now!" and An will release me.
77 This woman will carry off   the manhood of Lugalanne.

78 Mountain (and?) flood   lie at her feet.
79 That woman is as exalted (as he)—   she will make the city divorce him.
80 Surely she will assuage   her heartfelt rage for me.

81 Let me, Enheduanna,   recite a prayer to her.
82 Let me give free vent to my tears like sweet drink for the holy Inanna!
83 Let me say "Hail!" to her!

(xi) The Indictment of Lugalanne(?)

84 I cannot appease   Ashimbabbar.
85 (Lugalanne) has altered the lustrations of holy An and all his (other
        rites).

---

79 [a]U_4: ì-; p: im-; [b]p inserts -an-; [c]U_4: uru^{KI}; [d–d]J: mu-na-; O and U_1: mu-un-da-;
    [e]U_1 and U_4 omit; [f]O, U_1, p, (and A?): tug$_4$?; [g]O: -en; U_4: -a.
80 [a]O, T, and q: -ni; [b]p: -e-dè.
81 [a–a]D, O, and p: -mu; U_1 omits; [b]O: -na-; D: -un-na-; [c]D: -bé.
82 [a]A: -me-en.
83 [a]U_4: -hu; [b]O, J, U_1, and U_4: -ni; D: -un-ni-; p and q: -ne?-; [c]D: -ra-; U_4
    omits; [d]D, O, U_1, and p: -ba; U_4: -bar-re; [e]D, O, and p: -zu; U_4: -?; U_1
    omits; [f]O: -na; D: -un-na-; [g]D: -bé?
84 [a]p: AN.DU; [b]X: babbar-re; [c–c]So O, Y, p, (and U_4!); X: an-na-; s: an!-; U_1:
    nam-; D: nu-; [d]O adds: -en.
85 [a]D: -nir; [b]O (and J?): -ka; s omits; U_4: -ta; J: -gim?; Y: -na-ka; [c]U_1, U_4, p,
    and s: -na-; [d]D: -a-ni; s omits?; [e]O and U_1: ì-.

86 an-da é-an-na   ha-ba^a-an^b-kar
87 an-lú^a-gu-la-ta^b ní ba^c-ra^d-ba-da-te

88 é-bi la-la-bi ba-ra-mu-un^a-$^+$gi$_4$^{b} hi-li-bi^c ba-ra-mu-un^d-til

89 é-bi hul^a-a   hu^b-mu-di^c-ni-in^d-ku$_4$^{e}

[iii] 90 ˙tab˙^{a} ^{b}mu-ši-in^b-ku$_4$-ra^c-$^+$ni^d muru$_x$^{e}-$^+$ma^f-né hu-mu-un^g-˙te˙^{h}

91 ^{da}sun^b-zi-mu^c lú hé^d-mi^e-sar-re^f lú hé-im^g-mi^h-in-$^+$dab$_5$^{i}-bé^j

(xii)

92 ki^a-zi-šà-^{b}gál-la-ka^b gá-e a^c-$^+$na^d-me-en
93 ki-bala-hul-gig^a-^{d}nanna-za-^{b}a-kam^b an-né^c ha^d-ba-ab^e-sì-mu^f

94 ˙uru^a-bi˙ an-$^+$né^b ˙ha-ba˙^{c}-ra^d-an^e-si-il^f-le^g
95 ˙^{d}en-líl-le   nam˙ ha-ba-da^a-ku$_5$-dè
96 dumu-ír-pà-da-bi   ama-né na-an^a-šed$_7$^{b}-e^c

97 nin a-nir^a ki-gar-ra^b
98 ^{giš}má^a-a^b-nir-ra-zu^c ki-^{d}kúr-ra^d hé-bí^e-in^f-˙tag$_4$˙^{g}
99 ˙šìr-kù˙-gá-ke$_4$^{a}-eš^b ì-ug$_4$-ge-dé-˙eš˙^{c}

86 ^{a}U$_4$: -ma-; ^{b}D, O, U$_1$, U$_4$, p, and q: -da-an-; S (and Y ?): an-da-an-.
87 ^{a}D: lugal-; ^{b}O, Y, and p: da; ^{c}U$_4$: ma-; ^{d}U$_1$: -re-.
88 ^{a}H and Y omit; ^{b}A and D: -gi-en; O, U$_4$, and p: -gi; J: gi-na; s: -gim; ^{c}D
    omits; ^{d}s omits.
89 ^{a}D, H, J, O, U$_4$, Y, q, and s: é-hul-; ^{b}D: na-; ^{c}H, J, O, Y, q, and s: -un-di-;
    D: -un-ba-; ^{d}D omits; ^{e}U$_1$: -gur; D: -gù.
90 Restored from J, O, U$_1$, U$_4$, and s. ^{a}H: dab$_5$?!; $^{b-b}$D: mušen-; ^{c}J omits; ^{d}from
    U$_1$ and U$_4$; H, J, O, X, s, (and p): -na; D: -a-ni; ^{e}s: nì-na-; ^{f}J and X omit;
    ^{g}H, U$_1$, U$_4$, and p omit; ^{h}D: ti.
91 ^{a}U$_1$ and n omit; ^{b}O: ù-sun-; ^{c}U$_4$: -dè-ni; O omits; ^{d}D, H, K, p, (and Y ?):
    hu-; ^{e}U$_1$: -im-íb; H (and p ?): -mu-; O: -im-mi-íb; D (and K ?): -mu-un-ní-;
    J: -im-; t: -[i]m-mi-in-; ^{f}H adds -en; ^{g}O omits; ^{h}U$_1$ and U$_4$ omit; ^{i}from D, p,
    (and H ?); U$_1$ (and K ?): -ib-dab; O and U$_4$: -íb-dab$_5$-; ^{j}H and U$_1$ add -en; p: ?.
92 ^{a}U$_4$: NIN; $^{b-b}$-gala$_7$-ke$_4$; ^{c}D, U$_4$, p, and s omit; K: an-; ^{d}X: GA.

86 He has stripped An   of (his temple) Eanna.
87 He has not stood in awe   of An-lugal

88 That sanctuary whose attractions are irresistible, whose beauty is end-less,
89 That sanctuary he has verily brought to destruction.

90 Having entered before you as a partner, he has even approached his sister-in-law.
91 Oh my divine impetuous wild cow, drive out this man, capture this man!

(xii) The Curse of Uruk

92 In the place of sustenance   what am I, even I?
93 (Uruk) is a malevolent rebel against your Nanna—may An make it surrender!

94 This city—   may it be sundered by An!
95 May it be cursed   by Enlil!
96 May its plaintive child   not be placated by his mother!

97 Oh lady, the (harp of) mourning   is placed on the ground.
98 One had verily beached your ship of mourning on a hostile shore.
99 At (the sound of) my sacred song   they are ready to die.

---

93 ᵃD: -dím; ᵇ⁻ᵇD, K, O, and U₁,₂: -ke₄-eš; H and s: -e-ke₄-eš; ᶜJ: -e; H: -na; ᵈJ: a-; ᵉD: -an-; ᶠD (and U₁,₂?) add -re.
94 Restored from O, J, and K. ᵃU₁,₂: urú; D: uruᴷᴵ; ᵇD, K, O, U₁,₂, s, and t: -né; H, J, and n: -e; ᶜU₁,₂: -pa-; ᵈH omits; ᵉH, O, and t: -ab; K, Y, and s omit; ᶠU₁,₂ omits; ᵍK: -i; J adds -me-en.
95 Restored from D, H, K, O, and U₁,₂. ᵃD, O, U₁,₂, (and J?): -da-an-; H, K, and Y: -an-da-; s omits.
96 ᵃD and U₁,₂ omit; ᵇH and K: -silim-; ᶜK: -ma.
97 ᵃU₁,₂, n, (and H?) add -ra; ᵇD and U₁,₂ add -àm.
98 ᵃD, K, O, U₁, U₂, n, s, and t: má; ᵇD and U₂ omit; ᶜD and J omit; ᵈ⁻ᵈh: kúr; s: NE.R[U]?; ᵉU₁,₂: -bi-; h omits; ᶠH, K, U₁,₂, and h: -ib-; D: íb; O omits; ᵍrestored from J, K, and O; D: -te; h: -tab; H: tug₄?
99 Restored from D. ᵃO omits; ᵇY: -éš; ᶜH, K, O, and U₁,₂: -en.

(xiii)

100 ·gá-e[a] ^{d}·nanna-mu   èn[b]-$^{+}$mu[c] ba-ra-bí[d]-·in[e]-tar·

101 ·ki-lul·-*la[a]   hé[b]-gul-gul-e[c]

102 [a]·^{d}aš-ím·[a]-babbar[b]-re[c]   di-mu ba-ra-bí[d]-du$_{11}$

103 ·bí-in·[a]-du$_{11}$ nam-mu[b]   *li-bí-in[c]-du$_{11}$ nam-mu[d]

104 ·ù-ma·-gub-gub[a]-ba[b]   é-ta ba-ra-*e$_{11}$[c]

105 ·sín^{mušen}-gim· ab[a]-ta ba-ra[b]-an[c]-dal-e[d] zi-mu *um[e]-mi-$^{+}$kú[f]

106 ki[a]-š·eg$_{x}$(GÍR)[b]-kur-ra-k·e$_{4}$[c]   bí-in-gá[d]-e[e]

107 aga[a]-zi-nam-·en[b]-na·   mu-da[c]-*an-^{d}*kar

108 gíri ba-da[a]-ra ma-an-sì   a-ra-ab[b]-*du$_{7}$[c] ma-ab[d]-du$_{11}$

(xiv)

109 nin-kal-kal[a]   an-né[b] ki-ága

110 šà-kù-*zu mah-a[a]   ki-bé *ha-ma-[b]gi-gi[b]

111 nita$_{x}$(MÍ.UŠ)-dam-ki-ága- ^{ad}ušumgal[a]-an(a)[b]-ka[c]

112 an-úr an-pa   nin-gal[a]-bi-me-en

113 ^{d}a-nun-na-ke$_{4}$-ne   gú-giš[a] ma-[b]r·a-an[b]-gar·-re-eš

114 ù-tu-ud[a]-da-ta[b]   nin-bàn-da-·me·-en

115 ^{d}a-nun[a]-na dingir-gal-gal-la[b]-e-ne[c] a-*gim[c] ba[d]-e[e]-ne[f]-diri-ga[g]*

116 ^{d}a-nun[a]-na-ke$_{4}$-ne [b]$^{+}$nundum-nundum[b]-bi-ta ki-[c]su-ub
     ma-ra-aka-ne[c]$^{+}$

---

100 Restored from U_2. [a]r: -A; [b]U_2: ul?-; [c]A omits; [d]O, U_1, and h omit; [e]O, U_1, and h: -an; D, H, and K omit.

101 Restored from O, etc. [a]O adds -a; [b]H, K, h, s, t, (and U ?) insert -ib-; O and n insert -íb-; $U_{1,2}$ inserts -bí-ib-; [c]O and U_1: -en; H: -e-en; U_2: -dè-en.

102 [a–a]Restored from H, J, K, O, and $U_{1,2}$; J: ^{d}nanna-; h: ^{d}AŠ-AN.DU-; n: ^{d}IM; [b]H: babbar$_{x}$(UD.UD); [c]H, K, and h: -e; $U_{1,2}$, n, and s omit; [d]H, O, P, and $U_{1,2}$ insert: -in-; n: -ši-ib-[. . .].

103 [a]U_1 (and A ?) omit; [b]J: -me; h omits; [c]U_1 omits; [d]h omits.

104 [a]$U_{1,2}$: -gub^{bu}-; [b]K adds -àm; [c]$U_{1,2}$: -è; H (and n ?): -an-è; P (and J ?): -è-en.

105 [a]U_1: ki-ab-; [b]U_2 omits; [c]U_2 omits; [d]H, K, P, U_1, U_2, n, and u: -en; [e]H, P, $U_{1,2}$, h, n, p, (and K ?): im-; J: um-; [f]A, P: -KA; h: -kú-e.

106 Restored from $U_{1,2}$ and h. [a]P: ki-giš-; J: giš-; H, K, $U_{1,2}$, n, and r: giš-ú; h omits?; [b]P adds $^{ha-ah}$; H, J, K, h, r, and u add: ^{ah}; [c]P: -kam; n omits; [d]so also J ?; H, P, $U_{1,2}$, n, and u: -du-; h: -kú-; M: -DUN-; [e]M, P, (and n ?): -en; H (and u ?): -e-en; $U_{1,2}$: -me-en.

107 [a]K: SU; H: MA; [b]h: -e-; [c]U_1: -un-da-; [d]u omits.

(xiii) The Indictment of Nanna

100	As for me, my Nanna	takes no heed of me.
101	He has verily given me over to destruction	in murderous straits.

102 Ashimbabbar   has not pronounced my judgment.
103 Had he pronounced it: what is it   Had he not pronounced it: what is
     to me?   it to me?

104 (Me) who once sat triumphant   he has driven out of the sanctuary.
105 Like a swallow he made me fly from the window, my life is consumed.

106 He made me walk   in the bramble of the mountain.
107 He stripped me of the crown .   appropriate for the high priesthood.
108 He gave me dagger and sword—   "it becomes you," he said to me.

(xiv) The Appeal to Inanna

109 Most precious lady,   beloved of An,
110 Your holy heart is lofty,   may it be assuaged on my behalf!

111 Beloved bride   of Ushumgalanna,
112 You are the senior queen   of the heavenly foundations and
                               zenith.

113 The Anunna   have submitted to you.
114 From birth on   you were the "junior" queen.

115 How supreme you are over the great gods, the Anunna!
116 The Anunna kiss the ground with their lips (in obeisance) to you.

---

108 ᵃU₂: -ad-; ᵇU₂ omits; ᶜU₁: -du₁₁; ᵈM, P, U₁,₂, h, n, u, (and J ?): -an.
109 ᵃJ, K, U₁,₂, f, h, and u add -la; ᵇn: -e.
110 M omits line. ᵃK, U₁, f, h, n, (and u ?): -àm; ᵇ⁻ ᵇK, U₁,₂, h, n, and u: -gi₄-gi₄.
111 ᵃ⁻ᵃK, U₁, (and f): ušumgal; h: ušum-gal; ᵇso also M; P and U₁,₂: -an-na-;
    h (and f and n ?): -an-ki; K: na-x; ᶜP: -ke₄; h and n omit.
112 ᵃh omits.
113–14 Langdon's copy of A omitted these lines by mistake.
113 ᵃU₂ omits; ᵇ⁻ᵇh omits.
114–15 U₁ inverts these lines.
114 ᵃK, P, U₁, U₂, f, h, n, and u omit; ᵇU₂ omits.
115 ᵃn omits; ᵇK, P, U₁,₂, and f omit; ᶜ⁻ᶜU₁: E.NE; ᵈU₁: KU-; ᵉP: -en-; ᶠU₂ omits;
    M: -ne-en; ᵍn: -g[e]; U₂ (and f ?) omit.
115–16 h inverts these lines.
116 ᵃn omits; ᵇ⁻ᵇso P, U₁, and f; A, K, T, and h: du₁₁-du₁₁-; U₂: nundum-; ᶜ⁻ᶜfrom
    M and U₁,₂; P: su-ub ma-ra-ab-ke₄-ne; h: [su]-ub ma-ra-ke₄-ne; K: su-ub!ma!-
    x-y-x; A: x mu-ra-ab-su-ub-bu-*ta.

117   ˙di-n˙í^a-gá^b nu-mu-un^c-*til   di-kúr *di-mu^d-gim igi-⁺gá^e
                                                  ⁺mu^f-nigin^g

118   giš-ná-gi^a-rin^b-na^c   šu nu^d-um^e-mi^f-lá

119   du₁₁-du₁₁-ga-^dnin-gal^a   lú^b-ra nu-mu-na^c-búr^d

120   en-zalzale(UD.UD)-ga^a   ^dnanna-a^b-me-en

121   nin-ki-ága-an-na-^ame-en^a   *šà-zu ha-ma-šed₇-e^b

                                     (xv)

122   hé-zu^a-hé-za_x(ZU)^b-a^c-^dnanna   *za-a^f-kam bí-in^g*-du₁₁-ga^h
         lí-bí-in^d-du₁₁-ga^e

123   an-gim mah-^aa-za   hé-zu-àm^a

124   ki-gim dagal-la^b-^aza   hé-zu-àm^a

125   ki^b-bala^c-gul-gul-lu^d-^aza   hé-zu-àm^a

125a   kur-ra ˙gù-d˙é^b-^aza   hé-zu-àm^a

126   sag-giš-ra-ra^b-^aza   hé-zu-àm^a

127   ur-gim adda_x(LÚ-šeššig)-   hé-zu-àm^a
         kú^b-^aza

128   ˙igi-huš˙-^aa-za   hé-zu-àm^a

129   igi-huš-bi^b-íl-íl(i)^c-^aza   hé-zu-àm^a

[iv] 130   igi-gùn-gùn-na^b-^aza   hé-zu-àm^a

---

117 ^aU₂ omits; ^bU₂: -mu; l omits; ^ch: -ne-e; P, f, n, s, and u omit; ^dU₁: -mà-; ^eA: x; K omits; ^fA (and s?): hu¹-mu-; K, P, U₁,₂, and n: mu-un-; ^gU₁ adds -en; s (and U₂?): -nigin.

118 ^aU₁: -gi₄-; ^bh: -rí-; ^cu: -mà; ^dK omits?; ^eU₂ and q: im; K and s omit; ^fM, U₂, f, q, and s: -mi-in-; K and l: mu-un?; h omits.

119 ^aP, T, U₂, l, q, and s add -la; ^bU₁: lú-ulù_x-; ^cK, T, and q: -un-na; U₁,₂: -un-na-ab-; ^dU₁,₂: -bé; K (and A?): -bu.

120 ^aL: -ge?; ^bso also q; others omit.

121 ^{a–a}P, T, U₁, f, l, n, q, and s: -mu; ^bT omits; M, U₁, q, and s: -dè.

122 ^af adds -àm; ^bU₁: -za; ^cP, U₁, l, n, q, (and K): -àm, ^dP, T, f, n, q, and s omit; ^eK and q add -àm; ^fK adds -ni; n: -e-; ^gM, P, T, f, and n omit; ^hK and f add -àm.

123–31 ^{a–a}U₁: . . . -a-zu hé-za-àm.

124 ^bK, n, (and U₁): -la-a-; q: -a-.

125 ^bU₁ (and l and s?): kur-; ^cL and P: -ra; ^dU₁, b, n, and s omit.

125a First half of this line erased in A; restored from n. ^bl: -dé-a; s: -dé-e.

126 ^bK (and U₁): -ra-a-.

127 Traces in A; restored from f, l, (and T!); ^bK and P: -kú-ù.

117 (But) my own sentence is not con-   a hostile judgment appears before
     cluded,   my eyes as my judgment.

118 (My) hands are no longer folded   on the ritual couch,

119 I may no longer reveal   the pronouncements of Ningal to
                                man.

120 (Yet) I am the brilliant   high priestess of Nanna,

121 Oh my queen beloved of An,   may your heart take pity on me!

(xv) The Exaltation of Inanna

122 That one has not recited as a   that one has recited as a "'Tis
     "Known! Be it known!" of   Thine!":
     Nanna,

123 "That you are lofty as Heaven   be it known!
     (An)—

124 That you are broad as the earth—   be it known!

125 That you devastate the rebellious   be it known!
     land—

125a That you roar at the land—   be it known!

126 That you smite the heads—   be it known!

127 That you devour cadavers like a   be it known!
     dog—

128 That your glance is terrible—   be it known!

129 That you lift your terrible glance—   be it known!

130 That your glance is flashing—   be it known!

125–32 Order of lines differs in each exemplar, as follows:

A:	125	−125a	−126	−127	−128	−129	−130	−131	−132
c:	125	−125a	−127	−126	−128?	−130	−[		]
T:	125	−125a	−127?	−[					]
m:	[						]−131	−130	
q:	129	−132	−127	−126	−128	−125	−131	−[125a	−130]
n:	129	−132	−127	−126	−128	−130	−131	−125	−125a
l:	129	−132	−127	−128	−126	−130	−131	−125	−125a
s:	129	−[			]−130	−131	−125	−125a	
f:	129	−132	−130	−127	−126	−128	−131	−[125	−125a]
K:	129	−127	−126	−[					]
P:	128	−129	−132	−126	−131	−130	−127	−125a	−125
b:	[			]−128?	−132	−125	−125a	−131	
L:	[			]−125a	−125	−132	−131		
U₁:	128	−130	−129	−127	−126	−125	−131	−125a	

129 ᵇf omits; ᶜK, P, f, l, and n: -íl-i-.

130 ᵇU₁ omits.

131 en-na-nu[b]-še-ga[c]-[a]za   hé-zu-àm[a]

132 ù-ma[a] gub-gub-bu[b]-za   hé-zu-àm

133 [d]nanna li-bí[a]-in[b]-du$_{11}$-ga[c]   za-a[d]-kam b·í[e]-in·[f]-du$_{11}$-ga[g]

134 nin-mu íb-[+]gu[a]-ul-en[b]   aša [c]mah-[d]me-en[d]

135 nin-ki-ága-an-na-[a]me-en[a]   mir-mir-zu[b] ga-àm[c]-du$_{11}$

                              (xvi)
136 izi-ur$_5$ mu-un[a]-dub   šu-luh si bí-in[b]-sá

137 é[a]-éš-dam-kù ma-ra[b]-gál[c]   šà-zu[d] na[e]-m·a-še$_4$-dè·

138 im-ma[a]-si-im-ma-[b+]diri-ga-ta[c]   ·nin un-gal· *ma-·ra-[d]tu-ud[d]·

139 nì gi$_6$[a]-ù-na   ma-ra-an[b]-·du$_{11}$-ga[c]·
140 gala[a] an-NE-ke$_4$[?!b]   šu hu[c]-mu[d]-ra[e]-*ab-[f]·gi$_4$-gi$_4$·[f]

141 dam-díb-ba-za-ke$_4$[a]-eš   dumu-díb-za[b]-k·e$_4$-eš·

142 íb-ba-zu íb-gu-ul   šà-zu nu-te-en-te[a]

131 [b]U$_1$ and m omit; [c]U$_1$, m, n, q, and s omit.
132 U$_1$ omits line. [a]n omits; [b]f adds -dè.
133 [a]P omits; [b]H, P, b, and l omit; [c]H and b add -àm; [d]l: -e-; [e]P: KA-; [f]H, L, and
     l omit; [g]H adds -àm.
134 [a]A omits; [b]m: -e; [c]H, U$_1$, b, l, m, n, and s: ì-; P omits; [d-d]l and s: àm; P and
     n: -en.
135 [a-a]So also H; P, U$_1$, b, l, m, n, and r: -mu; [b]H, b, m, n, r, and s: -za; [c]P and
     s: -an-.
136 [a]H, P, U$_1$, l, m, n, and r omit; [b]H, P, U$_1$, l, and n omit.
137 Restored from H, P, and U$_1$. [a]P, U$_1$, m, n, and r omit; [b]H, U$_1$, and m insert
     -an-; [c]b adds -la; H: [g]ágar?; [d]n: -(eras.)-za; [e]U$_4$, b, and m: ha-.

131   That you are ill-disposed toward   be it known!
the . . . —

132   That you attain victory—   be it known!"

133   That one has not recited (this) of   that one has recited it as a "'Tis
Nanna,   Thine!'"—

134   (That,) oh my lady, has made you great, you alone are exalted!

135   Oh my lady beloved of An,   I have verily recounted your fury!

C. PERORATION

(xvi) The Composition of the Hymn

136   One has heaped up the coals (in   prepared the lustration
the censer),

137   The nuptial chamber awaits you,   let your heart be appeased!

138   With "It is enough for me, it is   oh exalted lady, (to this song) for
too much for me!" I have given   you.
birth,

139   That which I recited to you   at (mid)night

140   May the singer repeat it to you   at noon!

141   (Only) on account of your captive   on account of your captive child,
spouse,

142   Your rage is increased,   your heart unassuaged.

---

138   Restored from H. ^{a}U$_1$ and U$_4$ insert -an-; ^{b}A inserts [-ta-]; ^{c}r: -mu; $^{d-d}$P:
-dù; M, n, r, (and l?): -du$_{11}$.

139   Restored from P. ^{a}l, n, (and r?): -gi$_6$-a- (cf. line 56); ^{b}l: ab?; H and n omit;
^{c}H, M, U$_2$, n, and r add -àm; U$_1$ adds -me-en.

140   Restored from U$_1$. ^{a}U$_1$, l, n, and r add -e; ^{b}m and r: -ke$_4$; U$_{1,2}$: -ke$_4$-eš; U$_4$:
gá?; ^{c}U$_4$ omits; ^{d}U$_4$: ma; ^{e}U$_4$ omits; $^{f-f}$P: -gi-gi.

141   ^{a}u (and r?): -e-; ^{b}M: -za-a.

142   ^{a}M, P, U$_2$, and u add -en.

(xvii)

143 nin gú-tuku   nir-gál^a-gú-en-na-ke$_4$^{b}
144 sizkur-ra-na^a šu ba-an^b-ši-in-·ti·
145 šà-^{ad}inanna-ke$_4$^{b} ki-bé^c ba^d-na-ab^e-·gi$_4$·^{f}

146 u$_4$ ba-an-na-$^+$du$_{10}$^{a} ^{b}la-la^b ba-an^c-^{d}sù-sù^d hi-li-ma-^{e}az
    ^{f}ba-an^g-du$_8$-du$_8$^{f}

147 iti$_x$(U$_4$.^{d}NANNA)-è^a-gim^b ^{c}a-gim^c ^{d}la-la^d ba-^{e}an-gùr^e

148 ^{d}nanna u$_6$^{a}-zi-dè-eš ^{b}mu-un^b-è^c-a^d
149 ama^a-ni ^{d}nin-gal-la^b-ra^c šud$_x$(KA × ŠU) mu-^{d}na-an^e-
                                      rá^f-aš^g

150 giš-ká-$^+$an^a-na-ke$_4$^{b} silim-ma mu-^{c}na-ab^d-$^+$bé^e

(xviii)
151 nu-gig-ra du$_{11}$-ga^a-$^+$ni^b mah-a^c
152 kur^a-gul-gul   an-*da *me-^{b}ba-a^c
153 nin-mu hi-li gú-è ^{ad}inanna zà-mí^a

143 ^{a}U$_2$ omits; ^{b}Ū$_2$: -me-en; m (and u ?) add -ne; M adds -eš.
144 ^{a}P and U$_2$: -ni; U$_4$: -a-ni; ^{b}M, P, U$_2$, l, and u omit.
145 ^{a}B, P, U$_2$, U$_4$, l, n, and r insert: kù-; ^{b}B, P, U$_2$, l, and r omit; ^{c}m: -ba; ^{d}U$_4$:
    ha-; l: ga-; M, m, n, and r: ba-an-; ^{e}N omits; ^{f}restored from M, U$_2$, and l;
    P: -gi; m: -BI.
146 ^{a}A: -du$_{11}$; $^{b-b}$U$_2$: la; U$_4$: làl?; ^{c}M inserts -na-; $^{d-d}$P: -du$_8$-du$_8$; n: sù-ud?-sù;
    ^{e}U$_4$ inserts -RA-; $^{f-f}$M: ba-ra-mu-un-DU?; ^{g}l omits.
147 ^{a}B, P, U$_2$, l, (and U$_4$?) omit; ^{b}U$_2$, U$_4$, and l omit; $^{c-c}$B and P omit; $^{d-d}$U$_4$:
    làl?; n: la; $^{e-e}$A illegible; restored from P, U$_2$, and U$_4$; l and n: -gùr-ru.
148 ^{a}B: u$_4$; U$_4$: u$_6$-di-; l omits; $^{b-b}$r: ma-an-; ^{c}P and d: gub; u: ?; ^{d}P, U$_2$, l, n, r,
    (and u ?) omit.
149 ^{a}U$_4$ inserts -a-; ^{b}n: -àm; U$_2$: -e-; l: -ke$_4$; B and P omit; ^{c}M, U$_2$, U$_4$, l, and m
    omit; ^{d}U$_2$ inserts -un-; ^{e}P and U$_2$ omit; ^{f}U$_2$: rá-a-; P: -du$_{11}$; ^{g}P, l, (and u ?)
    omit; $^{e-g}$r: DU-šeššig?

(xvii) The Restoration of Enheduanna

143 The first lady,	the reliance of the throne room,
144 Has accepted her offerings	
145 Inanna's heart	has been restored.

146 The day was favorable for her, she was clothed sumptuously,	she was garbed in womanly beauty.
147 Like the light of the rising moon,	how she was sumptuously attired!

148 When Nanna appeared	in proper view,
149 They (all) blessed	her (Inanna's) mother Ningal.

150 The (heavenly) doorsill	called "Hail!"

(xviii) Doxology

151 For that her (Enheduanna's) speaking to the Hierodule was exalted,

152 Praise be (to) the devastatrix of the lands, endowed with me's from An,

153 (To) my lady wrapped in beauty, (to) Inanna!

---

150 ^{a}From U_2; A, B, U_4, d, l, and u omit; ^{b}M: -ka; ^{c}P and U_2 insert -un-; ^{d}n omits; ^{e}A adds [-en].

151 ^{a}n omits; ^{b}A: -bi; U_4: -a-ni; ^{c}P, T, n, and r: àm.

152 ^{a}P: kur-kur?; ^{b}P, U_4, (and l?) insert -da-; ^{c}P omits; n and r: -àm.

153 $^{a-a}$Separate line in A, $U_{1,2}$, U_4, n, and u.

Colophons. A: šu- nigín 2 šu-ši 33 mu-šid-bi

      x y z

      šu lugal-hé-à[m]

      dumu é-a-i-din-n[am?]

   B: šu ^{d}nin-urta-mu-*b[a-li-iṭ]

      igi ^{d}nisaba igi $^{din[gir}$ha-ià]

      hé-en-[ša$_6$]

   T: e-li-tum

   d: ^{1d}[. . .]

CHAPTER 3

Textual Questions

In the above chapters we have treated the composition as a whole, regarding it as a valid eyewitness account and interpretation of historical events of the early Sargonic period. But this reconstructed whole has come down to us in the form of separate manuscripts, dating, presumably, some five to six hundred years later. These manuscripts are valid testimony in their own right, especially to certain scribal conventions and educational practices which are not without significance for the cultural history of their own time. Therefore it seems justifiable to present the textual evidence separately and in some detail.

THE TEXTUAL REPERTOIRE

(see also the charts below, chapter 4)

A = CBS 7847   Published by S. Langdon, *PBS*, *10/4* (1919), 3; joins X, Cf. Plates 1–3.

B = CBS 7878   Ibid., 4.

C = MIO 1167   Publ. by Langdon, *BE*, *31* (1914), 41; collated by S. N. Kramer, *JAOS*, *60* (1940), 249; joins H.

D = AO 6713   Publ. by H. de Genouillac, *TRS* (1930), 51.

E = CBS 7924A   Publ. by E. Chiera, *SEM* (1935), 102A.

F = CBS 13313   Ibid., 104.

G = CBS 8507   Ibid., 105.

H = Ist. Ni. 2755   Publ. by Kramer, SLTN (1944), 64; joins C.

J = Ist. Ni. 4202   Publ. by Muazzez Çığ, *Or.* N.S. *22* (1953), Pl. L.

K = IM 49117   Publ. by J. J. A. van Dijk, *Sumer*, *11* (1955), Pls. viii f.

L = Kich C. 13   Publ. by de Genouillac, *Kich*, *2* (1925), Pl. 5.

M = Ist. Ni. 9667   Publ. M. Çığ, Haticé Kızılyay and S. N. Kramer, *Türk Arkeoloji Dergisi*, *8* (1958), Pl. XXXVI.

N = YBC 4656   Publ. below, Pls. 4–5.

O = YBC 7169   Publ. below, Pls. 6–7.

P = YBC 7167   Publ. below, Pls. 8–9.

Q = YBC 4671   Publ. below, Pls. 10–11.
R = CBS 1688   Unpubl.
S = Collection A. Smit (Amstelveen, Netherlands)
     No. 10 (courtesy K. R. Veenhof).
                   Publ. below, Pl. 12.
T = CBS 8528   Unpubl.
U_1 = U. 7750   Publ. by C. J. Gadd and S. N. Kramer, *UET 6/1*
                   (1963), 107.
U_2 = U. 16900A Ibid.
U_3 =   Ibid., 108.
U_4 = U. 16879F Ibid., 109.
U_5 =   Ibid., 110.
W = CBS 29.13.535 Unpubl.
X = CBS 29.15.422 Joins A; cf. photographs below, Pls. 1–2.
Y = IM 44336   Publ. below, Pl. 3.
Z = Ist. Ni. 4075 To be publ. in a forthcoming volume by Çığ,
                   Kızılyay, and Kramer.
a = Ist. Ni. 4207 Ibid.
b = Ist. Ni. 4367 Ibid.
c = Ist. Ni. 4458 Ibid.
d = Ist. Ni. 9660 Ibid.
e = 3NT 302   Unpubl.
f = 3NT 438   Unpubl.
g = 3NT 444   Unpubl.
h = 3NT 469   Unpubl.
i = 3NT 471   Unpubl.
j = 3NT 498   Unpubl.
k = 3NT 540   Unpubl.
l = 3NT 637   Unpubl.
m = 3NT 686   Unpubl.
n = 3NT 721   Unpubl.
o = 3NT 718   Unpubl.
p = 3NT 781   Unpubl.
q = 3NT 412   Unpubl.
r = 3NT 425   Unpubl.
s = 3NT 574   Unpubl.
t = N 4102   Unpubl.
u = N 1210–27   Unpubl.

We are greatly indebted to Samuel Noah Kramer for providing us with casts, copies and photographs of unpublished exemplars of the hymn which he identified in the University Museum, Philadelphia, in the Museum of the

Ancient Orient, Istanbul, and in the finds of the third (postwar) expedition to Nippur, and to Thorkild Jacobsen for graciously ceding his publication rights to the last-mentioned group of texts (e–s).

For previous treatments of lines 1–79 of the composition (based on A and B), see S. Langdon, *PBS, 10/4* (1919), pp. 260–64, and M. Witzel, *Keilschriftliche Studien, 6* (1929), 73–89.

TYPOLOGY OF THE MANUSCRIPTS

In view of the large number of exemplars (on the significance of which see above, page 4) it seems worthwhile to offer a brief summary and typology of the manuscripts, thereby illustrating the differences between an advanced literary text and the textual situation in respect to lexical lists, personal-name lists, and proverbs, which presumably were used at a more elementary level of instruction, and for which Landsberger, Chiera, and Gordon respectively have surveyed the textual typology admirably.[1]

Except for the most fragmentary ones, the surviving exemplars of the text can nearly all be assigned to one of five categories representing, in all likelihood, successively less polished products of the Old Babylonian scribal schools.

1. Prisms, complete in four columns of about forty lines each (R, l, and possibly o). These prisms, all from Nippur, probably constituted models for dictation, but in their present fragmentary state they cannot serve as a basis for our edition.

2. One-tablet recensions complete in four columns of about forty lines each. These are reliable texts from Nippur (A + X, B, C + H, T, n, q, r, s, u) and Ur (U_1,[2] U_2, U_3). We have chosen one of them (A + X) as the basis of our edition.

3. Three-tablet recensions in six columns (two per tablet) of about twenty-five lines each. This category, like the next two, includes texts from various sites. On the basis of their preserved text, they may be distributed with some probability as follows:

a. Tablet I   N (1–51)   W ([1]–60+)
b. Tablet II   O (52–102)   J (58–111)   D (51–100)   t (51–101)
c. Tablet III   P (102–end)   M ([104–end])   L ([100–end?])

4. Five-tablet recensions in ten columns (two per tablet) of about fifteen lines each, here pictured as follows:

a. Tablet I   Z (1–40)   e (1–41)   g (1–31?)
b. Tablet II   E (35?–70?)   Q (31–66)

---

1. E. I. Gordon, *Sumerian Proverbs* (1959), pp. 6–10 and the references ibid., p. 7, n. 15.

2. This is a more elongated tablet with three columns of about fifty lines each and the fourth column uninscribed except for the "explicit."

c. Tablet III U₄ (64?–92) Y (80?–105?)
d. Tablet IV K (91–128) b (108?–138?) f (106–132)
e. Tablet V c (123–end) m (123?–end)

5. Extract tablets of thirteen to twenty-one lines each. One cannot really regard these as recensions. They were clearly schoolboy exercises and include some of the worst orthography (for example, S). Some of them divide the text normally over obverse and reverse (h and probably U₅) but most of them have fewer lines on the reverse than on the obverse (S, i, j, k, p) and one of them leaves the reverse entirely uninscribed (a). Arranged as a hypothetical "series," they appear as follows: a (1–13), j (19–38), k (38–57), S (35–63), i (57–78), p (78–92), h (97–118), U₅ (137?–end). It is not difficult to picture the examples from the classroom(?) at Nippur (a, j, k, i, p) as the daily pensum of advanced students.

Theoretically, one might expect to find a still smaller unit, the exercise tablet, typically lenticular in shape, with a one- or two-line quotation from the composition. The fact that these have not turned up so far may simply prove that the text was not used at an elementary level of education, and that there was accordingly no need to resort to such tablets, which were most popular for lexical texts and proverbs, though also attested occasionally for royal hymns.

The same explanation may apply also to the distribution of the exemplars. These are not concentrated in the first part of the poem, as was often the case with more elementary texts, and in later periods with all texts. Thus the observation "that the first tablets of important series are preserved in many more copies than the following tablets" and that, consequently, "the apprentice scribe was apparently not required to complete his copy of the series before moving on to the next text of the prescribed curriculum"[3] does not seem to apply here.

A number of fragments from Nippur (F, G, d) are too small to be definitely assigned to any of the five attested categories, though they no doubt belong among them; it is even possible that they may prove to join some of the larger Nippur fragments such as C + H or T.

GENEALOGY OF THE MANUSCRIPTS

"The process of recension, i.e. constructing a stemma or pedigree," is a standard preliminary technique in the treatment of classical and medieval manuscripts[4] which has been applied, so far, to but a single Sumerian composition: the Sumerian King List in the edition of Thorkild Jacobsen.

3. A. L. Oppenheim, *Ancient Mesopotamia* (1964), p. 243. Cf. also the attestation charts below, in Chapter 4.
4. René Wellek and Austin Warren, *Theory of Literature* (3rd ed. 1963), p. 60.

It would be tempting to employ it on the numerous exemplars of nin-me-šár-ra, but this attempt has not been pursued to its conclusion here. We will content ourselves with suggesting the likeliest division into, and assignment to, "families" of manuscripts, and with drawing some conclusions from the resulting distribution.

Without becoming overly mechanical, we will approach this problem by means of what may be called "patterns of variants."[5] That is to say, we will concentrate, in the first instance, on variations between manuscripts that occur not just once but at repeated and preferably scattered intervals. By this means the danger of a chance scribal variation is minimized and a pattern emerges; at the same time a larger number of manuscripts is involved in the comparison than only the ten or twelve available for any one given line. The variant-patterns selected for this purpose here may serve at the same time as a check on these claims.

1. -za vs. -zu. Throughout the first part of the poem, a hymnic exordium to Inanna, the second person possessive pronoun appears as -za ($<$ zu + a [or ak]) in one group of manuscripts, and as -zu ($<$ zu + e [or zero]) in another. The pattern is nearly unbroken, as this table shows:

Line	-za														-zu														
8			N			R		e	g		n		r		A						T	U_2(+-šè)							
27	A	C	N		U_3	W		e	g		n			s								$U_{1,2}$							
32	A		N	Q	U_3			e				q										U_1			l	n			
36	A		N	Q	U_3			e		j	n	q								S		U_1							
37	A		N	Q	U_3			e		j		q								S		U_1							
38	A		N	Q				e		j		q								S		U_1					n?		
39	A		N	Q				e				q								S		U_1	Z?			n			
52	A	E			T	W								u		D		O	R	S		U_2				n			t
53a					T	W								u	A	D	E	O	R	S		U_2				n		s	t
53b	A															D?		O		S?				W?		n			t

This pattern is harder to trace in the rest of the poem where, moreover, many of these same manuscripts are no longer represented. But we find an interesting echo of it in the "magnificat" of lines 123–32, where -zu occurs, not as the second person possessive suffix, but as the verbal root "know." The distribution, however, as far as the manuscripts already noted above are concerned, is the same: word-final -za in A (here represented by the join X), -zu in U_1. At the same time the word-medial form has the opposite distribution: -zu- in A + X, -za- in U_1. The same pattern of variants holds throughout the eleven to twelve lines of the chorus, also for the other manuscripts preserved at this point (including L, T, b, f, l, n), all of which accord with A.

2. -mu vs. -me-en. A rather conspicuous variant for the copula of the

5. Cf. already a similar approach by Kramer, *AS, 12* (1940), 8–14, and M. Civil, "The Transmission of Sumerian Literary Texts" (unpubl. lecture); cf. *JAOS, 83* (1963), 400.

first person (-me-en) occurs at four scattered points of the poem in the form of -mu, as follows:

Line	-me-en					-mu								
67	A	C	J	U_2 U_4	D O									
81	AX		J	U_4	D O				6				p	
121	A		K?			P	T	U_1	f	l		n	q	s
135	A	CH	K			Q		U_1 b	l	m		n	r	

Although the pattern is not as pervasive in this case, it is never violated.

3. an-né vs. an-e and an-na vs. an-a. The patterning of this variant is considerably less consistent, due in part, though not entirely,[7] to the divergent ways in which the different manuscripts treated the distinction between an + e = "by An" and -an + e as part of the proper name Lugal-anne.

Line	an-né						an-e		an-na	an-a	Remarks
74	A CH D	J	O			s			U_1		Lugal-anne
75		D	O	U_1			A CH J				
76		D	O	U_1			A CH J				
77	A	D	O		U_4			U_1			Lugal-anne
93	AX	D	K O	U_1		s		J	CH		
94		D	K O	$U_{1.2}$		s t	CH J	n		AX	
109	A		K	P $U_{1.2}$	h	u		n			

This will become clearer if we rechart the pattern to indicate the degree to which the proper name is distinguished from the divine name, that is, the degree to which, most likely, the proper name was understood as such. Then we see that the number of verses in which the divine name is orthographically distinguished from the proper name is, in D and O, zero (out of a possible maximum of four attested occurrences). By contrast, it is three (out of five) in A + X, four (out of four) in C + H and J, and five (out of five) in U_1. No judgment is possible in the case of K, P, U_4, h, n, s, t, and u.

4. As a final criterion we will use, not a pattern, but a single variant of a conspicuous sort such as is least likely to have developed independently in separate manuscript traditions. In line 76, A and U_4 have an imperative, du_{11}-mu-na-ab (thus repeating the imperative of the preceding line), whereas five other manuscripts (D, H, J, O, U_1) have an indicative (ba-an-na-ab-bé, etc.).

6. U_1 omits the suffix here.
7. For an-e/an-né as a "free variant," cf. e.g. Kramer, *AS, 12* (1940), 8, n. r.

To sum up, the variant patterns (1) and (2) are fairly or even highly consistent within themselves, but they do not wholly agree either with each other or with the nonpatterned variants (3) and (4). Another table will make this graphic (with the less decisive patterns italicized):

(1)	A	*C*	*E*		N	Q	R	*T*		*W*	e	g	j	q	*A*		D	E		O		R S T U_1 U_2 *W* *Z*		l	*n*
(2)	A	C		J K		U_2 U_4											D		O P Q			T U_1		b f l m n p–s	
(3)	A	C		J		U_1 U_2											D			O		T U_1			
(4)	A					U_4										C	D		J O			U_1			

The extent of the "patterning of the patterns" is apparent in this arrangement. It must be granted at once that the arrangement is deliberately chosen and not the only possible one. But no grouping can put all the same manuscripts in the same columns, and the one chosen at least succeeds in respect of three manuscripts, namely A, D, and O, with A always falling into a different group from D and O.

We have already seen reason to regard A as a reliable manuscript (above, page 38) and we may now add that this argues for its antiquity, or rather for the antiquity of its prototype. On internal grounds it is even more obvious that D is a late manuscript. The other manuscripts fall between these two presumed extremes. Some, like C, J, and U_4, more often than not accord with A, others, like U_1, more often accord with D (and O). Still others go as often with one as with the other. Very approximately, then, we may chart the major families as follows:

A family: AX CH J K N U_3 U_4 e g j
Mixed family: E Q R T U_2 W n q r s
D family: D O P S U_1 Z b f l m p

An interesting corollary of this conclusion, no matter how tentative, is the observation that the family distribution seems independent of the provenience of the manuscripts, for exemplars from both Ur and Nippur figure equally in all three families. To put it another way, there are no conspicuous scribal peculiarities in the texts, either of Ur or of Nippur or, for that matter, of Kiš, though the single witness from that site (L) barely figures in the above comparisons. This finding implies a unity of the scribal system of education among the indicated centers, and at the same time a diversity in the manuscript tradition[8] that was quite independent of the provenience, though it may have been dependent on the date, of the individual copy.

8. For this, note also the arrangement of lines 125–32, which differs in every attested manuscript. Observe, however, that there is a definite tendency to have lines 125 and 125a at the beginning and lines 129 and 132 toward the end of the chorus in the "A family" (A and, apparently, c; T and m are too fragmentary) and vice versa in the "D family" (n, l, f, P, b, U_1; cf. also q, s, K, and L).

PLACE IN THE CANON

The question of the larger context can be disposed of quickly, since the evidence is meager and inconsistent. The usual mechanical criteria for assigning a place in a putative canon or sequence of literary texts[9] are entirely absent in the case of nin-me-šár-ra, and its place in the catalogue texts from Nippur[10] and Ur[11] is evidently determined by other considerations. We can only repeat what we have said above (pages 39, 3 f.) in other connections. On the basis of the, largely negative, evidence of the manuscript typology, the hymn probably belonged to an advanced stage of the curriculum of the scribal schools in general. More specifically, and on internal evidence, it probably formed an integral part, and perhaps the concluding part, of a cycle of hymns to Inanna which also included, at a minimum, in-nin-me-huš-a and in-nin-šà-gu₅-ra.

9. Cf. Hallo, *IEJ, 12* (1962), 22–24.
10. No. 4 out of sixty-two entries; cf. Kramer, *BASOR, 88* (1942), 14.
11. No. 8 out of fifty-five titles; cf. Kramer, *RA, 55* (1961), 171.

CHAPTER 4

Poetic Structure

The poetic structure integral to every Sumerian composition needs to be taken into account for its proper understanding.[1] It has been incorporated in the preceding transliteration and translation, and it remains at this point only to indicate the degree to which the suggested structure finds support in the texts.

The usual division of each line (or stichos) into two (or occasionally three) more or less equal parts (hemistichoi) is attested for nearly all but the longest and most crowded lines by one or more exemplars, usually, though not always, in agreement with each other. We have indicated the attested caesuras in our transliteration without, however, deeming it worthwhile to record conflicting witnesses.

After the stichos, or colon, the next highest unit is the bicolon or tricolon, that is two or three lines united by sense or structure or both to form a strophe. Such units are not mechanically indicated with anything like the rigor of the stichoi, but they played a role in the division of the text over separate tablets, as Falkenstein has seen,[2] and perhaps even over the separate columns of single tablets. The strophic structure suggested by our edition is based in the first instance on poetic and syntactic context, but may be tested against these more mechanical factors in over fifty cases (ll. 18–145). As the following charts show, nearly half of these are "confirmed" by one, two, or even more witnesses,[3] or thirty-five cases in all, as against only six cases where they are contradicted by the division into tablets and twelve where they disagree with the division into columns.

The tables will, however, show with equal clarity that the combination of couplets and triplets, most often four in number, into stanzas as proposed here finds no particular support in the external appearance of the texts.[4] It is

1. Cf. already H. Zimmern, *Sumerisch-babylonische Tammuzlieder* = *SSGW*, *59* (1907), 203 f.; P. Witzel, passim.
2. *SGL* 1:9 f.
3. As indicated by the "arrowheads."
4. This is true only of the *"kirugu"*-compositions, where the separate stanzas (*kirugu's*) are always respected in the tablet division in the sense that exemplars from multitablet recensions always contain one or more complete kirugu's.

based entirely on the internal evidence of the content and structure of the poem, and is intended to further its understanding, without claiming to restore an original feature of the composition. The same reservation holds for our proposed division of the entire poem into three "rhetorical" parts. Both of these divisions will, therefore, be defended in the literary analysis that follows.

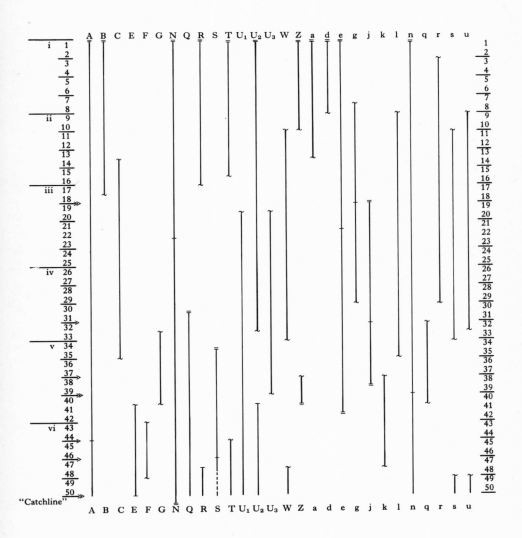

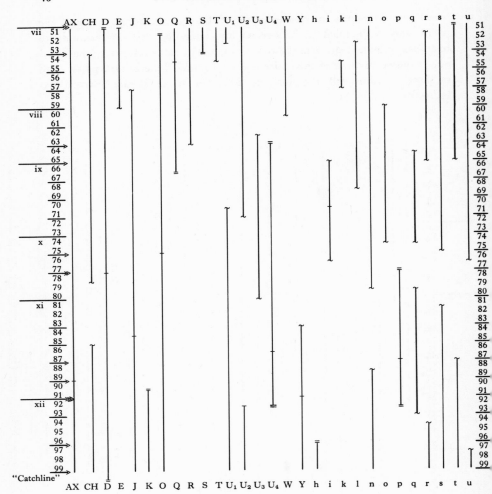

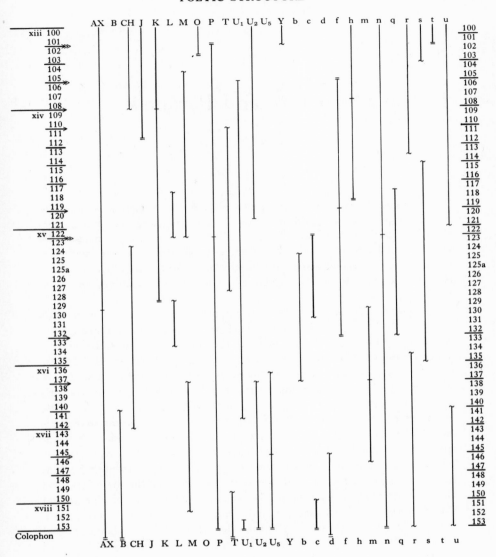

CHAPTER 5

Literary Structure and Parallels

The poem begins with a long exordium of sixty-five lines together constituting a paean of praise to the goddess Inanna. The numerous epithets and descriptions are, however, carefully selected to illustrate those characteristics of the goddess which are pertinent to the narrative that follows. They are, moreover, arranged in a conscious sequence—worthy of an Amos—in which the range of Inanna's activities is brought ever closer to the (presumable) audience of the poem.

(i) In the first stanza, then, Enheduanna speaks in general terms of Inanna's claims to all the great me's, a word which we will leave untranslated for the moment. Inanna's preoccupation with the me's may almost be said to approach the character of an obsession in Sumerian literature. In "Inanna and Enki" we have one version of the manner in which, with a good deal of deviousness, the goddess acquired the me's from Enki or, in Kramer's terms, "transferred the arts of civilization from Eridu to Uruk."[1] In "Enki and the Organization of the World" we have another, according to Falkenstein[2] later, treatment of the same theme, though here it is Enki who seems inclined to cheat the goddess out of her rightful share of the me's. Finally, our poem seems to revert to the same subject. There is no mention here, as in the mythology, of Enki. Rather it is An who bestows the me's here, and this is an act of grace, as it were. The verbs used to describe his donation of the me's are "give" (sì, line 14), and "bestow" (ba, line 152), rather than "distribute, assign" (ha(1)-ha(1)) as in the myths. Only a variant of line 64 (see the Glossary, s.v. túm) recalls the mythological version of Inanna's rape of the me's.

1. S. N. Kramer, *Sumerian Mythology* (2nd ed. 1961), p. 64; cf. Kramer, *From the Tablets of Sumer* (1956), pp. 91–96; *The Sumerians* (1963), p. 116.

2. A. Falkenstein, *ZA*, *56* (1964), 45 f. Cf. also the role of the Amorites in lines 129 f. and 245 f. of that composition. For the post-Akkadian date of literary references to the Amorites (Martu), cf. Falkenstein, *CRRAI*, *2* (1951), 16. The repeated references to Enki's dàra-abzu boat recall the date formula Šu-Sin 2.

The contexts in which me-ba (or me-si, me-túm) and me-ha(l)-ha(l) occur are quite revealing in this respect. The basic sense of ha(l)-ha(l) was established as "deal out" by Falkenstein,[3] who also called attention to the similar term ba, "apportion," in connection with the me. But a comparison of their respective contexts shows that me-ha(l)-ha(l) is most often modified by zi, "right, proper, just," and typically belongs in the sphere of Enki,[4] of whom we know, thanks to "Enki and the Organization of the World," that, as "bookkeeper of heavens and earth" (l. 71), he assigned appropriate functions to thirteen (lesser) gods, probably on behalf of Enlil from whom he here receives the me's (and nams; cf. ll. 61–66). On the other hand, me-ba (or me-si, me-túm) is characteristically found in the context of kinship symbolism, with An (or Enlil) bequeathing the me's to his divine offspring, or with a deity bestowing the me's on his or her divine parent.[5] In any case, the implication is of an "act of grace" on the part of the donor, not of a legal claim on the part of the recipient, and it is precisely this distinction that sets off our hymn from the myth of "Enki and the Organization of the World."

Since the me's occupy the present poem so prominently both at its beginning and its conclusion, one is inclined to suppose that they also form a, if not the, main concern of the body of the composition. And indeed we find them referred to again in the concluding couplet of the exordium (ll. 64 f.) in which Enheduanna begs leave to "recite the me's" of the goddess. Is then the whole argument which follows such a recital? Hardly all of it, but only its climactic, concluding part, the chorus in stanza xv. It is true that the elements of this chorus are not there called me's as such. But some of them, at least, are known as such from the catalogue of me's in Inanna and Enki. Moreover, these elements *are* here described as "'Tis Thine's" of Inanna, and the much longer list of such "'Tis Thine's" in Enheduanna's other hymn of praise to Inanna clearly coincides in large measure with the me's of Inanna and Enki. In short, the attribution to Inanna of these me's represents the main point of both of Enheduanna's hymns.

What, then, are the me's? This question, so long debated, has recently been summarized in a study according to which the me represents a more

3. *ZA*, *49* (1949), 125.

4. Cf. [nin]-nam-tar-re me-zi-h[al-hal-la] dingir-gal-gal-e-ne-šè (Falkenstein, *ZA*, *49* [1949], 106, l. 10); ub-šu-ukkin-na me-zi-hal-hal-ta (var.: -hal-ha-zu) (*VS* 2:8 i 26 = YBC 9838:21, unpubl.); ᵈen-ki ... me-zi-hal-ha-(la ᵈ)a-nun-ke₄-ne a-rá-bi ság [nu-di] (YBC 4620 = 7205: Hallo, *JAOS*, *88* [1968] in press).

5. A. Sjöberg, *Nanna* (1960), pp. 37 and 117, n. 112. In monumental texts, too, ba normally means bestowal by a superior upon an inferior, but is occasionally used in the opposite sense; cf. Hallo, *HUCA*, *33* (1962), 17. For a different notion, cf. Römer, *SKIZ* 129:22 f. and 153 ad loc.

primitive stage in, and the conception of an anthropomorphic deity (dingir) the most advanced stage of, a linear intellectual development.[6] The essential distinction between me and dingir, however, is not historical at all but better expressed as the relationship of *pars:totum*. For one of the most consistent and conspicuous features of the me's is their plurality or, in terms of the individual me, its partialness. No dingir can be equated or, in Sumerian terms, satisfied with a single me, but it is precisely the mark of a great deity that he collect or gather numerous me's to himself. The distinction can be phrased in more familiar theological terms as that between the deity and his attributes. It is therefore preferable to regard the me's as "divine attributes," and our poem as exalting Inanna by recognizing in, that is attributing to, the goddess those divine attributes that are hers by grace of An, the supreme god, with whom she is thus equated at the expense, not of Enki, but of Nanna.

(ii) From the preceding it is clear that the second stanza is closely related to the first, which already anticipated the familiar title of Inanna: Hierodule of An (nu-(u8)-gig-an-na). This epithet, though occasionally applied also to other goddesses[7] such as Nanâ and Ninisina, is most often used of Inanna. The translation "hierodule" is, however, ill-suited to convey its theological implications, for we know from the earliest Sumerian royal inscriptions that it was a high title, if not in fact the throne-name, of the queen-consort of Mesannepadda.[8] For Inanna, it therefore already implies that elevation to equal rank with An which is the point of the whole poem.

The significance of this claim is not, however, exhausted by its theological interpretation. We have suggested above that the invocation of and reliance upon Inanna by the Sargonic kings was intended at the same time to justify their imperial designs on Sumer (pp. 6–10). In this framework, it was in their interests to emphasize their adherence to Sumerian norms and beliefs. The "Sargonic theology" therefore represents Inanna, or the kings of Akkad acting in her name, as merely carrying out the commandments of the supreme deity of the Sumerian pantheon, An (l. 15).

(iii) The next stanza repeats this theme (l. 19) and develops it further. For if Inanna is to be executrix of An's commands, what then is the role of Enlil, the executor of An's commands in the traditional Sumerian view? The poetess implies that, as beloved of Enlil (l. 18), Inanna is, as it were, merely assisting him in his functions. And she remains quite willing to invoke Enlil for specific interventions such as the curse of Uruk (l. 95).

6. K. Oberhuber, *Der numinose Begriff ME im Sumerischen* (= *Innsbrucker Beiträge zur Kulturwissenschaft*, Sonderheft 17 [1963]). [The critique and alternatives proposed in this paragraph are my own. For van Dijk's views, see in detail his review, *OLZ*, 62 (1967), 229–44. W.W.H.]

7. Cf. Römer, *SKIZ* 294, n. 59 and below, Glossary, s.v.

8. Hallo, *Titles*, p. 30 and n. 6.

But Inanna's mission is not to be justified solely by this piece of sophistry. She claims a special capacity which equips her to discipline mankind. She is, in fact, the "Inanna of battle," a figure familiar not only from the bal-bal-e hymn sometimes so designated[9] but from numerous later allusions to the particular delight she takes in the sights and sounds of conflict.[10] These descriptions recall the Sumerian goddess of love and fecundity much less than the Akkadian Ištar and her warlike West Semitic cognates, Aštarte and Anat.

(iv) More specifically, we meet Inanna here (l. 27; cf. already ll. 17 f.) as the winged goddess, the flying Inanna who, in the guise of the storm(god), pounces on every unsuspecting culprit among the sinful nations. This metaphor, though employed here most dramatically, is not unique to our poem. In "The Curse of Agade" (l. 64), the goddess is described as "flying out of her city to give battle," according to two unpublished duplicates from the Yale Babylonian Collection.[11] In a late bilingual text from Babylon we read, in a description of her warlike pastime: "in the battle I fly like a swallow, I heap up heads that are so many harvested rushes."[12] Nor was this picture drawn exclusively in words: the much debated "Burney relief" shows the goddess with feet and wings of a bird,[13] a recurrent iconographic theme which is readily explicable on this basis.[14]

If the vengeful Inanna is, then, pictured as a kind of bird, it is not hard to see how, by extension, she could be compared to the storm, or even the stormgod Iškur. For the notion of the storm or storm cloud as a bird with outspread wings was a commonplace in Sumerian iconography as well as literature. Here, however, we are dealing with more than a simile. The "comparative" postposition (-gim), used in line 28, and the "comitative" postposition (-da), used in lines 29–31, often have more than merely metaphoric or instrumental force in religious texts. They may imply actual or virtual identification. This is a point that requires further study.[15]

The final couplet of this stanza (ll. 32 f.) is difficult to link with what precedes. One could perhaps translate: "At your feet the widow is 'seated,' she recites a lament with the harp of mourning" and treat it as alluding to the slaughter that Inanna causes in battle. But the notion of a tireless Inanna playing an instrument of mourning is known from "Enki and the Organization of the World" (ll. 441–43), and we therefore prefer to leave the subject of the couplet unchanged. One may also consider the possibility that Enheduanna alludes to herself in line 33, and that the "song" (i-lu) mentioned here

9. *SRT* 9:1–21; cf. M. Lambert, *RA*, *55* (1961), 193, No. 55(!)

10. B. Landsberger, *WZKM*, *56* (1960), 121 f. (b); ibid., *57* (1961), 23.

11. uru(KI)-ta mè-šen-šen im-ma-ra(da)-an-dal.

12. *SBH* 56 rev. 43 ff.

13. H. Frankfort, *AfO*, *12* (1937–39), 130.

14. For further parallels, cf. E. D. van Buren, *AfO*, *11* (1936–37), 354–57; Marie-Thérèse Barrelet, "Les déesses armées et ailées," *Syria*, *32* (1955), 222–60.

15. For -gim see a forthcoming Heidelberg dissertation on Sumerian metaphors.

refers to the four stanzas that follow. In any case, the hymnic exordium reaches a definite caesura here, at its midpoint, and the tenor of its second half if quite different, for it brings the terrible goddess into closer and closer touch with the world of the audience.

(v) That Inanna is supreme among the gods had already been expressed or implied in many ways in what preceded. Here, her supremacy is painted in graphic terms borrowed from, or at least shared with, the language of incantations, one of the oldest of all attested Sumerian literary genres (cf. above, p. 6). While Inanna swoops down like the great stormbird, the lesser gods flutter off like so many surprised bats. We meet here, for the first but by no means last time in the poem, the notion of Inanna's untamable anger. The translation "reins and heart" does scant justice to the conceptual range of the Sumerian idiom (ur_5-šà), which approximates respectively the emotional and intellectual responses.[16] Divine rage is, of course, a theme common to many Sumerian and Akkadian myths and epics, for natural and political disasters were quickly interpreted as the price paid to placate the divine displeasure.

(vi) An illustration of this lesson is provided in the next stanza, where a mountain (probably Ebih) is the unfortunate target of Inanna's wrath. Of the several, somewhat obscure allusions employed here, one (1. 45) is particularly suggestive. Large-scale slaughter involves the problem of disposing of the bodies of the slain, and even in our own days a river is sometimes considered the handiest receptacle for this purpose,[17] with dire results for the health of the survivors. The same idea is expressed elsewhere, not only in the rich Akkadian literature of the "wrath of gods,"[18] but more especially in the Sumerian myth of Inanna and Sukkaletuda. The "blood plague motif" found there by Kramer[19] is built around the filling of the wells with blood—though it is the wells of Sumer that are alluded to in that case. There may well be further connections between this, largely unpublished, composition, and ours (cf. especially 1. 90), as there certainly are between both of them and "Inanna and Ebih." The question is only whether the present stanza alludes, as in Sukkaletuda, to Sumer or, as in "Inanna and Ebih," to Ebih. In view of the mountain (hur-sag) of line 43, we incline to the latter view.

(vii) In any case the next stanza brings matters closer to home. Whether the unnamed "city" of line 51 is actually Uruk, as assumed here, or some other city, the reference is almost certainly to a Sumerian city. For Inanna

16. Cf. M. Civil, *Studies Presented to A. Leo Oppenheim* (1964), p. 69 and n. 6, and Hebrew KLYT WLB.

17. In December 1965, reports from Indonesia indicated that pollution of streams had resulted from massacres there.

18. Cf. e.g. Erra IV 38 f.

19. *ArOr, 17/1* (=Hrozny, *AV, 1* [1949]), 404.

appears here in purely Sumerian guise—as goddess of love and patroness of fecundity for man (l. 55)[20] and beast. The graphic representation of the holy stall (tùr, l. 54) with the symbol of Inanna belongs to the oldest Sumerian pictorial repertoire.[21] This sacred stall may even have served as a kind of "lying-in hospital" for women.[22] The ritual and cultic importance of Inanna, like that of her devotee Enheduanna, is thus brought into the argument at intervals throughout the poem (cf. ll. 68, 118 f.).

(viii) The proemium concludes with the invocation of Inanna. Once more the goddess' principal attributes pass in review: her rightful possession of the me's, her exaltation to highest rank, her wisdom, righteousness, sovereignty over nations and bestowal of fertility among men. A new one is added, however: Inanna is the "great lady of ladies," that is the greatest lady or, perhaps, more specifically, "chief queen" (of An).[23] We prefer the last translation because it is foreshadowed in the aforementioned "hierodule" title (above, p. 50) and because it has a counterpart in lines 112–14 where Inanna is referred to as the great nin of the heavenly foundation and zenith, and as the little nin from birth on; but nin-banda, "little queen," second queen, princess, is almost certainly a courtly title in the human sphere.[24]

The exordium concludes as the poetess for the first time steps forth in the first person (l. 63) and asks leave to recite Inanna's "holy hymn," which is equivalent in the parallel couplet to reciting her me's (above, p. 49). The "holy hymn" (šìr-kù) is probably a terminus technicus rather than just a pat poetic idiom, for the expression occurs frequently in juxtaposition with (šìr)-nam-šub "incantation (song)" and has itself possibly the connotation of incantation, as indeed šìr, "song," by itself seems at times to have. Moreover it passed into Akkadian as a technical term, širkugû.[25] It recurs in our text (l. 99) in a context which is anything but trivial. It is possible that in its present context it already heralds the climactic chorus that is to conclude the body of the poem.

---

20. Our translation reflects the apparent double entendre of ad-gi₄-gi₄ which, like šà-kúš-ù, can imply both "taking counsel" and "consorting together." For šà-kúš-ù, cf. Römer, *SKIZ* 174 ad *6:103 and 194 ad *6:191. For both verbs together, cf. Falkenstein, *SGL*, 1:18, 133.

21. Cf. e.g. E. Strommenger, *The Art of Mesopotamia* (1964), Pl. 23.

22. Cf. VAT 8381 (unpubl. inim-inim-ma a-ru-úh-tum) 1–3: mí-e é-tùr amaš-kù-ga im-da-an-zé-eb-ba-na / é-tu-ud-gála é-tùr amaš-kù-ga im-da-an-ze-eb-ba-na / numun-zi nam-lú-ulu_x šà-ga ba-ni-in-ri: "to his wife whom he had impregnated in the stall, the holy sheepfold, whom he had impregnated in the birth house, the stall, the holy sheepfold, in her lap he deposited the life-giving seed of mankind."

23. Cf. bēlit bēlēti, a favorite epithet of Inanna-Ištar in Akkadian contexts.

24. Hallo, *Titles*, p. 32 and nn. 2–4.

25. Cf. Glossary s.v. šìr-kù, and van Dijk, *SGL*, 2:98.

Another interpretation, however, is preferable. Since the "cohortative" ga-preformative is translated by the Akkadian (first person) precative in Old Babylonian texts,[26] it is possible that it came to share also the latter's asseverative function; a very similar development in Sumerian can be observed, probably under the influence of Akkadian, in the case of the (third person) "precative" preformative ha. The two functions may even have been secondarily differentiated, with the asseverative function employing the *hamṭu* stem of the verb and the cohortative one the *marû* stem, as in the case of the precative.[27] Both in the present passage and in line 135, the former is employed; in both cases, the form closes a major section of the poem. It is therefore preferable to regard it as referring to the recital that has preceded rather than to the narration that follows. Much the same can be said of Inanna and Ebih, where the comparable ga-i-i[28] concludes rather than precedes the hymnic apostrophe to the goddess.

(ix) Even if we maintain the cohortative meaning, it is clear that the sacred song to which Enheduanna refers does not follow at once. Instead, the second part, or Argument, of our poem begins with a long recital of Enheduanna's past glories and present plight, partly narrative and autobiographical, and not all addressed to Inanna. But this too can be paralleled from other contexts, for the "recitation of the exaltation" is a fairly common topos not confined to Inanna, and not always followed at once by the apostrophe to the deity even when the "cohortative" form of the verb is used.[29]

The argument begins, as we interpret it, with Enheduanna's banishment from Ur, on the assumption that the *gipāru* of line 66 is the famous "cloister" or residence of the high priestess of Nanna in that city or possibly at Karzida or Gaeš, and not the synonymous residence of the (male) en at Uruk, whose existence Jacobsen has pointed out.[30] Enheduanna recalls two highlights of her quondam priestly functions at Ur (l. 68). The carrying of the ritual basket is not, here, an allusion to the office of canephore which may or may not have been filled, at times, by women,[31] but rather to the bringing of grain and other offerings, in a ritual basket, to Bau and other deities in an as yet somewhat obscure rite. Gadd has gathered the evidence from scattered sources

26. Cf. e.g. passim in the *OBGT*.

27. Cf. *SRT* 42:11: ka-tar-mu hé-si-il-le nam-mah-mu hé-em-me and below, note 29. Jacobsen, however, holds that ga "is incompatible with durative [i.e. *marû*] root," *AS, 16* (1965), 73.

28. Cf. e.g. *PBS* 10/4:9 obv. 23.

29. Cf. Glossary s.v. nam-mah ... du₁₁/e.

30. T. Jacobsen, *ZA, 52* (1957), 107–9, n. 32; cf. also *Enmerkar*, 60 ff.; *CAD,G*, 84cd. [The newly published Enheduanna text, *TMH* n.F. 4:7 ll. 107–68, clinches the argument in favor of Ur. Cf. especially l. 160: gi-ma-sá-ab ku₄-ku₄-dam asilá₄ di-dam.]

31. On this point, cf. C. J. Gadd, *Iraq, 10* (1948), 97; Hallo, *HUCA, 33* (1962), 11, n. 79.

and periods which shows that this basket was related to the "marriage" of Marduk, possibly with Bau, and has found pictorial representations which liken it to a shell. One of his literary references is worth quoting in full: "you, oh maiden Inanna, are not (yet) a woman! You are going to the house of the oneiromancer (*šā'ilu*); after having filled the ritual basket with barley, put it as food to his [i.e. Dumuzi's!] dead spirit."[32]

The acclaim (asila) in the same line (68) may be related to the preceding, for in at least one instance the term occurs precisely in the middle of a "fertility topos" contained in a hymn to Bau.[33] Although the exact significance of the high priestess' role as pictured here remains obscure, it does then seem to emphasize her importance to the rites connected with assuring fertility. This is in keeping with Enheduanna's other reminders of her own role and Inanna's (cf. above, p. 53).

Her present status is in stark contrast to these past glories.[34] The exact nature of her fate is again enveloped in poetic ambiguity, but it seems to involve her exile to the edin, the steppe, for that is where, from all indications, the "lepers' ward" (ki-sì-ga; euphemistic variant: ki-ša₆-ga, good place) is to be found. Occasionally it is also located in the marsh (ambar).[35] But here the steppe is surely meant, for the next couplet[36] evokes the picture of a sudden duststorm blotting out the light of day.[37] The reference in the next couplet (ll. 72 f.) is thus not the mud (ùh)[38] of the marsh but to the confusion (šu-ùh-a) and dust (sahar) in which Enheduanna wallows.[39]

(x) The next stanza is the first in which Inanna is not addressed in the second person. Rather she is spoken of in the third. We therefore take the divine name Suen in line 74 to be a vocative (in spite of the variant spellings in -e and -a) and regard the whole stanza as an address to the moongod.[40] As

---

32. *SBH* 77:29. Note also in a neo-Sumerian balanced account concerning fish, an entry for twenty baskets (of one gur fish each ?) described as the bride-price (nì-mí-ús-sá) of Bau (L.B. 2490, to be publ. in *TLB* 3/2–3).

33. Cf. Römer, *SKIZ* 237, l. 46.

34. The verbs in lines 66 and 68 are here regarded as preterites. Note the variants, especially the ending -em in line 66 (0), probably <-en; for J. Krecher's interpretation of final -e(n) <-àm after ku₄ and other verbs, cf. *ZA*, 57 (1965), 29 f.

35. See Glossary s.v. ki-sì-ga; cf. also J. Laesse, *Bît rimki* (1955), pp. 84 f., and van Dijk apud *Heidelberger Studien zum Alten Orient* (1967), 240–43.

36. Lines 70 f.; note the interesting climactic parallelism with the subject postponed to the second stichos.

37. For a similar contrast between light and shadow, cf. *Enmerkar*, 428 f.: u₄-ta gizzu-šè àm-è-e / gizzu-ta u₄-šè àm-è-e.

38. Assuming that ùh could stand for úh or uh = *ruttu*, for which see Deimel, *ŠL* 2:398:17; 2:392:8 f.

39. For synonyms to the last expression, see Glossary s.v. sahar ... gi₄.

40. Note that nam-mu occurs only in direct discourse; Falkenstein apud *MSL*, 4:42.

Enheduanna's nominal "husband and employer," he might be expected to intervene on her behalf against Lugalanne.

The reference, by name, to the hated usurper at Uruk is surprising in this context, though not more so than that to Mansium, who usurped Uruk under Naram-Sin, in the "Curse of Agade." [41] In fact, later copyists may no longer have recognized the name as such (above, p. 41). As to the identity of this Lugalanne, we have already referred to his place in the "historical tradition," (above, p. 9) where the spelling of his name varies between Lugal-an-né (Old Akkadian period) and Lugal-an-na (OB period). Neither of these spellings is, however, likely to mirror the original name in its full form. More likely it is a hypocoristic abbreviation of a name more fully preserved in the contemporary royal inscriptions or their later copies, or in the royal hymns. On this assumption, names like Lugalannadu of Umma,[42] or Uruk,[43] or Lugalannedu[44] or even Lugalannemundu of Adab suggest themselves for comparison. The "short" form of the name also occurs in the "Royal Correspondence of Isin." [45] But this is not the place to explore the historical implications of these possible identifications.

For the present, rather, much of the historical content of the entire poem remains concealed behind the difficult lines 77–79. The identities of subjects and objects, of the antecedents of the personal pronouns, of the "woman" of lines 77 and 79 and of the city in line 79—all are open to numerous interpretations. Perhaps the clue is in the verb of line 79a, "she is equally exalted, as exalted (as he)." As who? The whole tenor of the poem suggests: An! The force of the verbal prefix (i)n-ga-, with or without the corresponding nominal postposition -gim, is precisely that of a comparative (see the Glossary, s.v.), while the stem -mah is used in this poem with the particular connotation of exalt(ed) (cf. especially ll. 64, 123, 134). It would agree with the whole concept of the composition to read line 79a as "That woman (Inanna) is as exalted as he (An)," and to regard the "city" of line 79b as Uruk, the city of An, Inanna, and Lugalanne, with whom this stanza deals, and not Ur, the city of Nanna-Suen to whom the stanza is addressed.

The content of Enheduanna's plea is short and to the point. She begs Suen to intercede for her with An so that he may "release" her. The verb used

41. Falkenstein, *ZA, 57* (1965), 54, l. 68. Is there any connection with *si-ù-um* king of Gutium? Cf. V. Scheil, CRAI (1911) 319. [See Addenda 2.]

42. Ibid.

43. F. Thureau-Dangin, *RA, 20* (1923), 6.

44. Cf. CT 36:40:25 ff., translating "(Baba), you have given to Lugalannedu(g) the lofty name of Lumma" against Falkenstein, *SAHG* No. 9:49 ff. on the one hand, and Kramer, *BiOr, 11* (1954), 182, n. 19, on the other.

45. *PBS* 13:48 iii and duplicates; cf. now F. A. Ali, *Sumerian Letters* (Ann Arbor, University Microfilms, 1964), p. 105 (B 10:6).

(du₈) is perhaps intentionally ambiguous, implying release from imprisonment, while at the same time continuing the idiom of line 69, for it is typically used of the release from sin (nam-tag) as symptomized by sickness. But how is the moongod to help Enheduanna at Uruk if that city is ruled by a usurper who, as the next stanza suggests, has thrown An himself out of his temple? Enheduanna anticipates this objection: Lugalanne, she says, is not my legitimate sovereign, and though he may have An in his power, my goddess Inanna is of equal rank with An and will cause Uruk to throw off the yoke of the usurper. Translated into historical terms, then, the appeal to Nanna is an appeal to his city Ur to aid the Sargonic party in the suppression of the revolt of Uruk, or at the very least not to support the rebellion.

(xi) But Nanna is not to be appeased so easily (l. 84), nor Ur weaned away from its traditional alliance with Uruk (cf. above pp. 7–9). Enheduanna loses both her priestly offices, at Ur as well as Uruk, and therefore her "lines of communication" with both Nanna and An are broken. This is merely implied for the former.[46] For An it is more explicitly stated by reference to the cultic disorder caused at Eanna, the great temple of Uruk, by Lugalanne. The lustration was properly a function of the high priestess,[47] and Lugalanne has evidently turned this function over to a candidate of his own, perhaps his own sister-in-law. The full import of the crime (l. 90) is difficult to convey in a literal translation, but both verbs are used elsewhere in connection with sexual advances to the high priestess[48] or to adultery in general,[49] and the first (tab-ku₄, var. dab₅-ku₄) may be the hitherto unknown equivalent of *šutahhû* (*šuta"û*), "to make oneself a companion,"[50] which in omens and other contexts suggests the juxtaposition of two objects in general, and sexual violation in particular. Lugalanne even stands accused of destroying Eanna, a charge possibly supported by the archaeological evidence, for the excavations of the temple area have uncovered what R. North describes as a "vexing hiatus" in the entire Sargonic period.[51] Thus Enheduanna must turn back to Inanna, asking her to expel the convicted usurper (l. 91).

---

46. Line 84; Ašimbabbar is another name for the moongod; cf. lines 118 f. for the reference to a similar cultic disability with reference to Nanna's consort Ningal.

47. Cf. line 135 and van Dijk, *JCS*, *19* (1965), 9, ll. 199 f.: en šu-luh-kù me-bé šu bí-in-du₇-<a>. [Cf. now also *TMH* n F. 4:7 l. 117: šu!-luh nam-en-na-ke₄ si bí-[in-sá].]

48. Cf. J. Nougayrol, *JNES*, *9* (1950), 51; for a similar theme with reference to Inanna, cf. Kramer, *ArOr*, *17/1* (1949), 402 n. 14: giš im-ma-ni-in-du₁₁ / ne im-ma-ni-in-su-ub, "he cohabited with her, he kissed her."

49. Cf. E. Reiner, *Šurpu* II 47 f.: *a-na* É *tap-pe-e-šú i-te-ru-ub* / *a-na* DAM *tap-pe-e-šú iṭ-ṭe₄-hi*.

50. W. von Soden, *Or.*, *16* (1947), 437–49; *AHw*, 22b; Nougayrol, *RA*, *44* (1950), 28.

51. *Or.*, *26* (1957), 250. For An's epithet in line 87, cf. an-gu-la = ᵈ*A-nim* GAL-*ú* in IVR 18:2:13 f.: F. Delitzsch, *BA*, *10* (1913), 143 f.

(xii) The stanza that follows again poses the problem: who is addressed, and by whom? The clearest examples of the second person are "your Nanna" (l. 93) and "your ship of mourning" (l. 98)—and it is clearly Enheduanna who refers to "my Nanna" in the next stanza (l. 100). Apart from line 92, which begs the question, the clearest example of the first person is "my sacred song" (l. 99)—and in line 63, "your sacred song" surely referred to the sacred song of Inanna. One might thus incline to regard the entire stanza as Inanna's response to Enheduanna, heeding her appeal in line 91. In the next stanza, the introduction with an emphatic "as for me" (gá-e, l. 100) would mark the reversion to Enheduanna's first-person speech.

Two arguments speak against this interpretation, however. In the first place, the first 142 lines of the poem are otherwise one continuous address by Enheduanna. More important, the presumed vocative in line 97 ("Oh lady"), clearly attested in nine manuscripts, would have to be emended (to balag, tigi, or the like). We prefer, then, to regard "your Nanna" as alluding, in this case, to the fact that Nanna-Suen is the father of Inanna, and "my sacred song" as the song which Enheduanna sings to Inanna.

On this interpretation, it is Enheduanna who now invokes An and Enlil to call down a terrible curse upon Uruk. No other city can be meant in lines 92–96.[52] Though much briefer, it is something of a counterpart and fore-runner to the "Curse of Agade" (ll. 228–74). Most of its individual phrases can be found again in other contexts: line 96 in the Sumerian love charm,[53] line 97 in the "Lamentation Over Ur,"[54] and echoes of line 98 in the Inanna laments.[55] But the particular thought of the climactic line 99 is peculiar to the present context. Does it, and therefore the whole strophe, allude to the ritual entombment of a whole retinue together with the "queen" as attested by the famous pre-Sargonic graves excavated at Ur by Sir Leonard Woolley? This practice could still have been a living memory in the Sargonic period when these lines were written, but already forgotten by the Old Babylonian copyists, most of whom replaced the third plural form of the original text with a verb in the first person singular.

(xiii) The next stanza is the logical conclusion to the preceding three and begins, like those, with a mention of the moongod under one of his three names. He had been invoked in the first of these four stanzas, but the appeal

---

52. For ki-zi-šà-gál-la as epithet of Uruk, cf. Hallo, *BiOr*, *23* (1966), 243 (=YBC 9859):23, 25.

53. Falkenstein, *ZA*, *56* (1964), 116, l. 34; read against Falkenstein: nam-mu-un-šed$_x$ (MUŠ!.A!.DI!)-dè; cf. Falkenstein, ibid., 127 f.

54. Kramer, *AS*, *12* (1940), 26, l. 86.

55. *BL*, p. 71, ll. 18–26 and *SAHG* No. 33:12–15 (cf. above, p. 5); *JCS*, *16* (1962), 80: HSM 7522:6 ff.

fell on deaf ears because, presumably, Enheduanna was no longer his high priestess at Ur, while in Uruk he was unable or unwilling to take a stand against the rebellion of Lugalanne. In other words, Ur had failed to side with Sargon against Uruk. For Enheduanna, it makes little difference whether Ur openly sided with Uruk or merely observed a discreet neutrality (cf. l. 103); the effect is the same: she is now banished from Uruk to the "mountain" as previously from Ur to the steppe. Her life is "consumed" (l. 105).[56] The inhabitants of Ur add insult to injury, suggesting that Enheduanna kill herself, or immolate herself (and thus perhaps unfit herself for the resumption of her priestly duties) in the manner of the androgynous dervishes (kur-gar-ra) who are normally associated with "dagger and sword" (gíri-ba-da-ra; cf. the Glossary, s.v.). There is nothing left for Enheduanna but to turn to Inanna.

(xiv) The two long stanzas that follow represent the climax of the "argument" and of the poem as a whole. In the first, Inanna's epithets once more pass in review, including a brief allusion to her relationship to Dumuzi ((ama)ušumgalanna, l. 111). The rest emphasize her supremacy among the gods. Then Enheduanna recalls that her judgment has not been concluded (l. 117; cf. already l. 102); the passage is the first certain literary reference for the verbal form of the juridical term di-til-la, "finished judgment."[57]

In lines 118 f., the appeal is fortified by a significant allusion to still another function of the high priestess: her role as oneiromancer (ensi (EN.ME.LI) = šā'iltu). Apparently she ministered not only to Nanna at Ur, but also to his consort Ningal.[58] Ningal, like some other goddesses, is known as a patroness of dream interpretation, and the mention of the ritual couch (literally "fruitful, shining couch") suggests an incubation technique for eliciting the divine response.[59] The implication is that the inhabitants of Ur have only themselves to blame if these responses can no longer be revealed or interpreted (búr) to them.

The role divination played in Sumerian religion was much less pervasive than in Akkadian practice, but what evidence there is has recently been

56. The idiom is obscure, but one may compare such compounds as zi . . . ir, zi . . . DU, zi . . . du$_{11}$, and zi . . . bal-bal, for which see the Glossary, s.v. zi-kú.

57. Cf. Falkenstein, NG, 1 (1956), 10, n. 3 and possibly SEM, 58 iv 17 (=Marriage of Martu 124): u$_4$ ba-te-a di nu-til-le [. . .]. For the earliest di-til-la, cf. now T. Donald, MCS 9/1 (1964), No. 250.

58. Cf. already Figulla, "Offerings in the Ningal-temple at Ur," Iraq, 15 (1953), 88–122, 171–92, with many references to the en-priestesses; cf. esp. pp. 188 ff.

59. Cf. A. L. Oppenheim, The Interpretation of Dreams (=TAPhS, 46 [1956]), 221 ff.). The various meanings of šu-lá (below, Glossary) point to a semantic parallel with Proverbs 6:10 = 24:33: "a little sleep, a little slumber, a little folding (ḥbbq) of the hands to rest."

elucidated by Falkenstein.[60] He has assembled the literary allusions to the king's function as hepatoscope (máš-šu-gíd-gíd) or oneiromancer (ensi) and to the role of goddesses in incubation. While there are no exact parallels to the high priestess serving in this connection, it is at least worth noting the relatively large role that dream interpretation played in the attested examples of Sumerian divination, compared to its relatively modest role in the vast repertoire of later mantic techniques.[61]

(xv) In the great "magnificat" that follows, the poem reaches what we venture to consider its title theme. Here Enheduanna fulfills her wish to "recite the me's" and to attribute them, not to Nanna but to Inanna, thereby exalting her to equal status with An (see above, pp. 49 f.). Both hé-zu-hé-za$_x$(zu)-àm[62] and za-(a)-kam are types or elements of liturgical compositions (see already above, p. 4), as is clear from the references collected in the Glossary (s.v.). Judging from the intentional alternation of "u" and "a" in the designation of the former as well as in the chorus itself (for which see above, p. 40), the liturgy was probably sung antiphonally.[63]

The first two lines of the chorus (ll. 123 f.) particularly merit attention, for they are found in this same position in all the manuscripts, whereas the remaining nine lines (in some cases ten lines) are arranged in different, and apparently arbitrary, order in every attested exemplar. They are not therefore solely a variant version of the familiar saying "who is tall enough to reach heaven, wide enough to embrace the earth."[64] Rather, the first line, in and of itself, is equally open to the translation "that you are (as) exalted as An—be it known!" Almost certainly, this connotation was intended by the poetess, at the least as a double entendre, as the conclusion of the chorus (l. 134) indicates.

But the couplet has still another level of meaning. For the comparison with heaven and earth implies at the same time the combination of astral and terrestrial character peculiar to the goddess in later descriptions. Here, in fact, is the historical point at which these two contradictory characterizations are first united in the one deity. She owes her astral nature (as the planet Venus)[65]

---

60. "'Wahrsagung' in der sumerischen Überlieferung," apud *La Divination en Mésopotamie ancienne . . . XIVe Rencontre Assyriologique Internationale* (1966), 45–68. Note also that Sukalletuda "observed and studied various omens in order to carry out the divine ordinances"; Kramer, *ArOr, 17/1* (1949), 401.

61. Perhaps we may even see a distant and legendary echo of the princess-diviner in certain Jewish and Hellenistic traditions (sometimes linked to Berossos) which regarded the daughter or daughter-in-law of Noah as the first Sibyl.

62. Cf. *SLTN* 61:174–83 for a similar chorus in honor of Ninurta. Here the refrain is . . . -za nu-uš in-ga-zu-àm, "that you . . . —would that it were also known."

63. For another type of antiphonal (?) chant, cf. Glossary s.v. lum-a-lam-ma.

64. For this millennial topos in Sumerian and Akkadian literature, cf. Hallo, *IEJ, 12* (1962), 20, n. 33.

65. For which see, e.g., Römer, *SKIZ*, 169 ad Iddin-Dagan *6:87.

to Ištar; but her claim to the role of earth goddess is based on her identification, as Inanna, with Antum = ki, the terrestrial consort of the Heaven-god.[66]

What, then, is the relationship of our text to the later tradition of the exaltation of Ištar as attested by late bilingual texts from Uruk and Babylon in which the equation of Ištar and Antum is made explicit?[67] While this question must be left unanswered here, it is already possible to suggest that the later series[68] links up somehow with a much older tradition of which our poem is a contemporary witness. We therefore consider the verbs of line 134 as related to each other like the adjectives gal and mah,[69] that is as positive to comparative or superlative.

(xvi) The first stanza of the peroration is also the last in which Enheduanna speaks in the first person. In it, the poetess seems to describe her creative labors. Unfortunately the reference to the composition (l. 139) is not as explicit as one might wish, but perhaps the technical term for it is contained in line 135[70] which we have, without much conviction, appended to the preceding stanza. But the notion of giving birth to, or fashioning[71] in connection with intellectual activity or creativity is attested in the concept of "conceiving the word."[72]

As Enheduanna relates it, then, her inspiration came to her by night, and was cast into poetic terms in a creative agony well-phrased as labor pains. Nocturnal inspiration is, of course, not confined to poets. It is thus, for example, that Gudea conceived or received, first the notion of building the temple of Ningirsu, and then the procedures to be followed toward this end—albeit in (successive) dreams which he himself was unable to interpret without

66. See also the Glossary s.v. nin.

67. F. Thureau-Dagin, "L'exaltation d'Ishtar," *RA, 11* (1914), 141–58 = *TCL* 6:51 f.; S. Langdon, "A Bilingual tablet from Erech of the first century B.C.," *RA, 12* (1915), 73–84. Cf. also the neo-Assyrian "Hymn to Ištar as the Belit of Nippur" from Nineveh, published under the name of S. Langdon, *AfK, 1* (1923, rep. 1938), 20–29 (rep. 12–18), and of M. Sidersky, *RA, 26* (1929), 21–30, and its neo-Babylonian duplicate from Sippar published by V. Scheil, *ZA, 10* (1895), 291–98; Falkenstein, "'Inannas Erhöhung'" *BiOr, 9* (1952), 88–92. What is the relation between Ištar's astral name (ᵈti-mú-a) here, the epithet nin-a-dè-mú-a attested on statues of Gudea to Geštinanna, and the divine name ᵈNin-DÈ-mú-a attested on a votive vase of [Nammahani?] of Lagaš (De Sarzec, *DC*, p. lix and Pl. 44ᵇⁱˢ3)?

68. Falkenstein, *BiOr, 9* (1952), 90 and *MDOG, 85* (1953), 11, dates the composition of this series to the late Kassite period.

69. For which see van Dijk, *SGL* 2:122.

70. Reading lù-lù (for ilula?) instead of the proposed mir-mir. Note also the parallel with line 121.

71. For the variation between (ù)-tu(d) and dù, cf. Hallo, *JAOS, 83* (1963), ad No. 35.

72. inim-mud-(gál); cf. van Dijk, *SGL* 2:114 f. and *JCS, 19* (1965), 12, l. 45.

further divine assistance. Nor does Enheduanna speak explicitly of a dream, but even if the scene in lines 136 f. is meant to describe the preparations for "incubation,"[73] she was presumably qualified to be her own dream interpreter (cf. above, p. 59).

At any rate, the passage is unique in Sumerian literature in describing the process of *poetic* inspiration. And though this (nocturnal) process can be reconstructed for Akkadian literature from the so-called "prayers to the gods of the night,"[74] the description of the process itself is unmatched there except by the strikingly similar denouement of the "Epic" of Erra. The parallel extends further, for just as Kabti-ilani-Marduk there recommends his "composition"[75] to future generations to protect them from a recurrence of the wrath of Erra which it describes, so Enheduanna concludes with the pious wish that the professional chanters may henceforth include her hymn in their repertoire. And just as the Erra Epic was, according to its author, recorded faithfully and literally,[76] so Enheduanna used the verb repeat ($šu \dots gi_4-gi_4$, see the Glossary, s.v.) in the, presumably, technical sense of repeating verbatim in connection with this wish.

The couplet that follows (ll. 141 f.), like the last line of the preceding stanza (135), is difficult to justify at this point. Perhaps the two "insertions"—if that is what they are—are related. Inanna has been appeased, her rage mollified. Why, then, any further need to pacify her wrath (l. 142) or recite her fury (l. 135; but cf. above, p. 61)? The allusion here may be to an entirely different aspect of the Inanna cult, perhaps to a preexistent Sumerian aspect such as is reflected in certain Inanna and Dumuzi laments.[77] If so, the poetess is merely acknowledging the goddess' claims on her traditional lamentations even while asserting her triumph in the particular circumstances described in her own poem.

(xvii) The denouement of our poem can be dealt with briefly. It can hardly be denied that the exaltation of Inanna implies at the same time the restoration of Enheduanna, their two fates being so closely linked that in lines 146 f. it is hard to decide whether the narrator, who takes over in this stanza, is speaking of the one or the other. In any case, Inanna accepts Enheduanna's prayers, and the change in her fortunes which are the result or (we might say) the

73. For the éš-dam in line 137, cf. Falkenstein, *ZA*, 56 (1964), 118 f.

74. Oppenheim, *Analecta Biblica*, 12 (1959), 282–301; Hallo, *IEJ*, 12 (1962), 19.

75. In Erra V 42 (cf. P. F. Gössmann, *Era-Epos*, pp. 36 f.; W. G. Lambert, *Iraq*, 24 [1962], 122 f.), he is styled the *ka-ṣir kam-me-šú*, "compiler of its tablets, author," just as the Collection of Temple Hymns (above, p. 3) is called, in the colophon, the "compilation (ka-kešda = *kiṣru*!) of Enheduanna."

76. Erra V 43 f.

77. Cf. V. Scheil, *RA*, 8 (1911), 162 f., 8 f., 19 = *VS* 2:2:6: dam-dab₅-ba-(a)-na dumu-dab₅-ba-(a)-na / dam-ug₅-ga-(a)-na dumu-ug₅-ga-na . . . / ga-ša-an-an-na mu-ut-na-tur-ra-na ír-gig ì-še₈-e.

symptom of this acceptance is as dramatic as the Job-like restoration of the "just sufferer" in "Man and his God" (ll. 118 ff.). The abrupt turnabout in the mood of the poem is paralleled by a syntactic reversal, for in this final stanza, probably for the first time in the poem (but see above, p. 58), Enheduanna is no longer the speaker. Even line 145, which in the form of an "optative" is a standard conclusion of Sumerian letter-prayers,[78] is phrased in the third person and as an accomplished fact. Whether all this entitles us to regard the entire stanza as an editorial addition is a question that may therefore legitimately be raised. It is the more germane as the "reconciliation" with Nanna or his consort Ningal (ll. 148–50) which, in effect, concludes the poem, is hardly in keeping with the role in which Nanna has been cast in the poem as a whole. But at this stage it is too early to attempt to answer such questions of higher criticism.

(xviii) The concluding doxology is, superficially, of the standard hymnic variety, and places our poem into the rather heterogeneous category of zà-mí-compositions (hymns of praise). Still, it has specific overtones beyond the usual platitudes. The divine epithets are again selected with reference to the particular themes of the composition (see especially above, p. 50, on "hierodule (of An)" and "inheritor of the me's" of An, and pp. 50 f. on the "devastatrix of the lands"). And the entire stanza conveys the sense of a goddess emerging triumphant from a disputation, much as in the concluding rubrics of an adaman-du$_{11}$-ga.[79] Here, as there, the whole stanza is composed of a nominalized subject of the type "for the fact that . . . ," whose predicate is "praise to the deity."[80] Here, as there, this doxology is preceded by a reconciliation of the principal contestants. All that is lacking is the divine or royal judgment and the symbolic payment to the victor, but then this feature, which is even found in the prose frame of the Book of Job,[81] is reserved to wisdom compositions. And if wisdom texts in general, and disputations in particular, may be said to concern themselves with "academic questions," that is far from the case with nin-me-šár-ra: it was the literary expression of a burning politico-religious reality by its author, princess to Sargon, priestess to Nanna, and poetess to Inanna.[82]

---

78. M. Civil, *Studies Presented to A. Leo Oppenheim* (1964), p. 89. On the letter-prayers and their intimate connections with the later ír-šà-hun-gá's, see a forthcoming study by Hallo, *JAOS, 88* (1968).

79. Cf. e.g. van Dijk, *Sagesse* (1953), p. 50.

80. Cf. also the concluding lines of "The Curse of Akkad" and "Inanna and Ebih"; Falkenstein, *ZA, 57* (1965), 124 ad 283.

81. Van Dijk, *Orientalia et Biblica Lovaniensia, 1* (1957), 15 f.

82. And we might almost add, in the light of lines 118 f., "prophetess" to Ningal.

CHAPTER 6

The Typology of Divine Exaltation

In the attempt to arrive at an overall evaluation of our text (above, Chap. 1), we stressed its historical and literary setting. Only in conclusion (esp. pp. 6–10) did we allude to its religious significance. Yet the text is, after all, primarily a religious document and, if we have not erred completely in reconstructing its historical context, it should be possible, indeed obligatory, to exploit its religious connotations as well. This will be attempted here in reference to that area where political and religious history meet. We would address ourselves, in short, to the question of the impact of historical events on the history of religions as reflected, subsequent to the exaltation of Inanna, in the later religious literature of the Ancient Near East.

But first we must dispose of an alleged antecedent. The chief deity of the Sumerian pantheon, An, is conspicuous by his absence from the archival and monumental texts of pre-Sargonic Lagaš.[1] Now a series of cones and tablets published since 1930 records Entemena's construction of the é-mùš for Inanna and her consort,[2] and the latter's name was read an lugal-é-mùš, An, master of the é-mùš, by M. Lambert, who then concluded that the inscriptions commemorated the introduction of the divine couple of Uruk into the cult of Lagaš upon the conclusion of the alliance between Entemena of Lagaš and Lugalkinišedudu of Uruk referred to in the concluding temporal clause of the clay cones.[3] This interpretation was vigorously challenged by C.-F. Jean,[4] and it must be given up. Indeed, it has now been demonstrated that the cones in question came from the site of Bad-Tibira, about halfway between Uruk and Girsu-Lagaš.[5] The original é-mùš is in

---

1. Note, however, in the onomasticon such names as Eannatumu.

2. See now E. Sollberger, *Corpus* sub Ent. 45–73, 74–75, and pp. xiii note (1) and xvi note *. Note also that the Oriental Institute has an unpublished brick (A 7121 = Ent. 15; cf. *JNES*, 17 [1958], 212, § 7) and bronze foundation figurine (A 7122) inscribed with two versions of an inscription of Entemena to ᵈLugal-é-mùš.

3. *RA*, 42 (1948), 191–97.

4. "Le dieu An à Lagaš," *RA*, 44 (1950), 127–33.

5. E. Crawford, "The location of Bad-Tibira," *Iraq*, 22 (1960), 197–99.

fact the temple of Dumuzi at Bad-Tibira,[6] and ^dlugal-é-mùš is therefore a name or manifestation of Dumuzi. As such it can even be written without the "divine determinative,"[7] as can the related dialectal name or epithet umun-é-mùš, "lord of the emuš."[8]

Thus the exaltation of Inanna at Uruk in the early Sargonic period remains for the present the first example of its kind attested in the literature. But there are later ones. In the first place we may cite those cases in which a deity is called "superior to An." The passages cited below (p. 73) show that this epithet was not confined to Inanna. And while it may have degenerated into a literary cliché by the time of Sin-iddinam, who applied it to Nanna (see below, p. 73), there are other instances where it seems to reflect more profound theogonic speculation.[9] The best example of this is the case of Nergal. In a fragmentary hymn edited by van Dijk,[10] his exaltation is expressed not only in these terms, but more specifically. Nergal here rules on behalf of An in the role customarily reserved for his father Enlil; he determines the fates for An and all the gods; he exercises the Enlil-ship (nam-^den-líl = *illilūtu*) in Uruk.[11] The reason for his elevation is given in vague terms which, however, seem to allude to historical circumstances: he has been credited with some sort of major victory in the mountainous lands at the rising of the sun (that is, in the east), and these enemies are described as [lú-s]a-gaz, that is bandits (*habbātu*) or perhaps murderers (*šaggāšu*)[12] or even Hābiru. It is impossible to identify these allusions more precisely, since the date of the composition is unknown, but it is unlikely to antedate the neo-Sumerian period, given the fact that Erra occurs in it (l. 36).[13] Perhaps we have here a reference to Utuhegal's victory over Gutium, the last great triumph of Uruk.[14] But the possibility cannot entirely be ruled out that the earliest Hābiru are here alluded to, and that they suffered a major defeat at the hands of a king who regarded Nergal as his personal or dynastic deity. On the basis of the royal inscriptions, the likeliest candidates, apart from Ari-šen of Urkiš and Nawar[15]

6. Cf. already (i.a.) A. Falkenstein, *ZA, 45* (1939), 186; *SGL, 1* (1959), 58 f.

7. Cf. e.g. Y. Rosengarten, *Le concept sumérien de consommation* (1960), p. 287.

8. Written ù-mu-un-e-mu-ša; cf. J. Krecher, *ZA, 57* (1965), 18 f. and n. 11.

9. The term "theogony" is used here, for want of a better, to suggest not only the genealogy and "birth of God," but also for the changing status, relative to each other, of various deities within a single pantheon.

10. *TCL* 15:26 = *SGL* 2:2; cf. now also van Dijk, "L'hymne à Marduk avec intercession pour le roi Abi'ešuh," *MIO, 12* (1966), p. 61.

11. On this difficult concept, cf. in detail ibid., pp. 59–74.

12. If we may read [(lú)-gi]š-gaz in spite of the collation.

13. For the "early history" of this deity, cf. van Dijk, *UVB, 18* (1962), 51; Gössmann, *Era-Epos*, p. 68; I. J. Gelb, *MAD, 2* (2nd ed. 1961), 55, no. 25.

14. So van Dijk, *MIO, 12* (1966), 62; cf. ibid., p. 74.

15. F. Thureau-Dangin, *RA, 9* (1912), 1–4.

and An-am of Uruk,[16] are the kings of Larsa, who repeatedly invoke Nergal as patron deity (lugal),[17] as personal deity (dingir),[18] or, what amounts to the same thing,[19] as divine begettor (dingir-sag-du[20] = *i-lum ba-ni qá-aq-qá-di*[21]). It must be admitted, however, that the early history of the deity,[22] as of the Hābiru,[23] is too obscure to admit of any facile correlation of the two.

The exaltation of Ninurta was, in essence, the theme of the lengthy myth called lugal-e u₄-me-lám-bi nir-gál whose popularity is attested by numerous Sumerian exemplars from Old Babylonian times and late bilingual versions from Nineveh, Kalah, Assur, Babylon, and elsewhere.[24] In certain formal respects, the myth parallels the later versions of the exaltation of Inanna, as pointed out by Langdon.[25] At first glance, the parallel does not extend to the contents, since the Ninurta myth takes place entirely in the realm of divine and natural phenomena, with no reference to human history; as Jacobsen has summarized it, "Altogether the myth of Ninurta and Asag appears to be a nature myth telling of the yearly battle of spring and winter."[26] But it should be remembered that, in its latest form, the exaltation of Ištar likewise preserves none of the allusions to contemporary history with which its Sargonic forerunner is replete. And although, in this form, it does not go back as far as the Ninurta myth,[27] we should consider the possibility that there was an earlier version of the latter myth as well. In it, such mythical matters as the great battle of Tablets II–V may have had a much more clearly historical background.

Perhaps the most celebrated example of the elevation of a Mesopotamian deity is that of Marduk, who rose from a completely obscure status to the most exalted rank in the pantheon. There is no question about his dramatic

16. Thureau-Dangin, *SAKI* 222a = Hallo, *BiOr, 18* (1961), 12 sub Sin-gamil 2.

17. Ibid., pp. 7–11 sub Abi-sare 1, 2; Warad-Sin 12, 13; Rim-Sin 12, 23.

18. Rim-Sin 12.

19. Hallo, *JCS, 20* (1966), 136 f., n. 53.

20. *UET* 8:85:23.

21. Kudur-mabuk I (cf. *CAD,B*, 94c).

22. For a recent survey, cf. J. B. Curtis, *HUCA, 28* (1957), 142–77.

23. Cf., in addition to the well-known surveys by J. Bottéro and M. Greenberg, also especially J. R. Kupper, *Les Nomades en Mésopotamie* (1957), Chap. 5, and Mary F. Gray, "The Hâbirū-Hebrew problem . . .," *HUCA, 29* (1958), 135–202. Note that the neo-Sumerian references to (lú-)sa-gaz listed in these studies and in Sollberger, *TCS* 1 (1966) No. 6, all use the term in its nonethnic sense of "robber." The same probably holds true for the Sumerian literary allusions, for which cf. Römer, *SKIZ* 50:224 and 72, n. 384.

24. See the bibliographical note by M. Lambert, *RA, 55* (1961), 185, No. 12.

25. *RA, 12* (1915), 73–76; but cf. Falkenstein, *BiOr, 9* (1952), 91 f.

26. *JNES, 5* (1946), 147.

27. See above, note 68 to Chapter 5.

climb in the divine hierarchy. The argument is only about when it took place. There is some evidence to suggest a date in the Late Old Babylonian period.[28] A recent study by W. G. Lambert proposes another solution.[29] According to him the ascendancy of Babylon under the Hammurapi dynasty is unmatched by references to Marduk's supremacy in any Old Babylonian sources, whether date formulas, personal names, royal inscriptions, or literary works, and there is no evidence to suggest a change in this situation through most of the Kassite period. Under the Second Dynasty of Isin, however, and in the reign of Nebukadnezar I (ca. 1124–03 B.C.) in particular, one can detect a sudden upsurge in the explicit "status" of Marduk in a number of sources. This "turning point in the history of ancient Mesopotamian religion" had been long in the making, but its immediate cause, according to Lambert, was the recovery of Marduk's statue from captivity in Elam, which he dates to this reign. Given the importance attached to the divine statues, their capture and recapture, throughout Mesopotamian history, the occasion alluded to could well have loomed large in Babylonian religious history. But we should not overlook the significance of this particular triumph over Elam for political and military history as well. For the defeat of Elam by Nebukadnezar ushered in, if not immediately then in short order, a total eclipse of Elamite power and the removal of this traditional rival from the Babylonian scene for almost three centuries.[30] The magnitude of the military triumph, then, may well have combined with the dramatic recovery of the statue to lay the basis for Marduk's exaltation at Babylon in the unique manner attested by the "Epic of Creation" and other sources.[31]

Since this example brings us well into the second half of the second millennium, it may be worth noting in conclusion the striking parallel that it affords to the "exaltation of Yahweh" at the Exodus, an event datable only a little earlier. The religious history of Israel is almost inexplicable without accepting the historicity of the Exodus, as most Biblical scholars are now inclined to do. But the Exodus gains in historical validity, not only by its

28. Van Dijk, *MIO*, *12* (1966), 57–74.

29. "The reign of Nebuchadnezzar I: a turning point in the history of ancient Mesopotamian religion," *The Seed of Wisdom: Essays in Honor of T. J. Meek* (1964), pp. 3–13.

30. R. Labat, *CAH*, I/II² fasc. 23 (1964), 23 f. For the relations between Isin II and Elam, cf. also Hallo, "Akkadian Apocalypses," *Israel Exploration Journal*, *16* (1966), 231–42, esp. 237 f.

31. Weidner's hypothesis that the Marduk cult had already reached its apogee in Assyria a century earlier, after the capture of Babylon by Tukulti-Ninurta I (see most recently F. Köcher, *ZA*, *50* [1952], 201 f.), should be weighed against the evidence of a much more gradual growth in the importance of this cult as attested primarily by personal names; cf. H. A. Fine, *Studies in Middle Assyrian Chronology and Religion* (1955), esp. pp. 108–12 (=*HUCA*, *25* [1954], 126–30).

continued literary reflection in the "Exodus typology" of later Israelite thought and experience, but also by its direct and intimate bearing on the emergence of Israel's God to an unchallenged supremacy in the eyes of his people. Events at the Reed Sea and God's exaltation are closely related, and this relationship, which deserves further study, can materially help to date the former while strengthening the historical character of the latter.

The phenomenon thus illustrated has many other ramifications for the history of religions, in particular for the problem of henotheism. There is no intention to go into these here, nor even to exhaust the examples of divine exaltation within the Mesopotamian experience. The illustrations already adduced, however, should suffice to emphasize the close dependence of major "theogonic" revolutions on historical events. We have tried to link the exaltation of Inanna to certain events in the Sargonic period as adumbrated in the poem nin-me-šár-ra. The later parallels, it is to be hoped, indicate that this historical aspect is a legitimate and fruitful one under which to view the phenomenon of divine exaltation not only in Mesopotamia but also elsewhere in the Ancient Near East.

CHAPTER 7

Glossary

Because of the lack to date of an adequate dictionary, or even glossary, of literary Sumerian, translations of Sumerian literary texts have in recent years either rested on unstated lexical assumptions or else called forth lengthy commentaries on each passage, in which basic lexical questions were intermingled with purely grammatical comments on the one hand and considerations of historical or literary significance on the other. Although such commentaries fulfill an extremely useful and, in the absence of dictionary or glossary, even an essential function, they tax both the commentator's time and the reader's. It has seemed to us more appropriate to segregate the purely lexical evidence by presenting it in simple alphabetical order and by citing in full the most cogent *Belegstellen* except where these have already been assembled conveniently by our predecessors.

The nature of the Sumerian literary idiom makes this the more feasible as certain words repeatedly appear in combination. This is true not only of the so-called compound verbs but of numerous other complexes peculiar to the stylized diction of Sumerian poetry. By concentrating on these complexes rather than the simple roots, it is possible to reduce the attested citations to those best suited to throw light on the specific meaning of the separate elements. This is not to ignore the frequent interchange in the elements of such complexes. But such interchanges, while contributing to lexical clarity, can better be treated in the framework of the "literary criticism" of the entire genre in which they occur, where their role is primary. Words and phrases already discussed in the commentary are therefore not repeated here.

a-a: *abu* "father." R-ugu, 52 = *abu ālidu.*

á: *idu* "arm, wing, strength." u_4-dè R . . . -sì, 17; á-ní-za, 27, perhaps = *ina ramāniki.* Cf. *NG 3*: 89 á-na "mit eigener Hand"; the expression is explained by a variant á ní-za dúb "flying on your own"; á ní-za seems to be an ellipsis for á-ní-za dúb.

á-ága: *wu"uru*; *tērtu*: "instruct(ion), decree." R-an-na, 19.

á-dúb: "to flap one's wings." á ní-za dúb, 27, "flapping (your) wings, (supported) on your own." For á-dúb, cf. *CAD,A*, s.v. *abru* B and D;

JNES, *12* (1953), 187, n. 78; *Enmerkar* 508: kin-gi₄-a mušen-gim
á-dúb ì-ak-e; *AS*, *12* (1940), 28, l. 106; cf. Jacobsen, *PAPhS*, *107*
(1963), 481, n. 24: mušen-an-na-gim R hé-en/em-ši-aka; cf. also
á-búr, "to open the wings," *CAD,A*, s.v. *abru* B and D, and *TLB*
2¹:1:4:20.

á-tuku: *bēl emūqi* "able-bodied." *See* guruš á-tuku, below.

ab: *aptu* "hole; hole serving as a window." Cf. ab-làl = *takkapu*, Landsberger, *JCS*, *8* (1954), 63, n. 144; R-ta . . . dal 105; cf. *SBH* 54 rev. 23 f.
(=*HAV* 3:8–9; *VS* 10:176:4 f.) tuᵐᵘˢᵉⁿ-ab-ba-ke₄ ab-làl in-šub-ba
a-bi dal-la-[x] = *su-um-ma-ta ap-ti ša ap-ti-ši-na id-da-a-ma e-ki-a-
a[m . . .]*; *ZA*, *57* (1965), 61, l. 222: tuᵐᵘˢᵉⁿ-bé ab-lál-ba še hé-ni-in-
ša₄; *ZA*, *57*, 115: tuᵐᵘˢᵉⁿ ab-lal-bi-ta ba-ra-an-dib-dib-bé-ne =
su-um-ma-ti ina a-pa-ti-ši-na i-bar-rù; *JNES*, *12* (1953), Pl. LXVII, l. 149:
tuᵐᵘˢᵉⁿ-gim ab-lal₄-ba ní-bi-a ad-e-eš ba-ni-íb-gi₄ and cf. *JNES*,
12, 176 f., 187, n. 78.

a-da-lam: *inannāma*, *MSL*, 4:64:7; *CAD,I*, 142 "now"; fixed verbal
form: i-dal(da-al)-àm = *inannāma*, ibid.; cf. *Enm.* 147: a-da-en
a-da-nun a-da-lugal; van Dijk, Sagesse, p. 31, n. 3: a-da-min;
R . . . du₁₁, 76.

ad-gi₄-gi₄: *mitluku*; *šitūlu*. Cf. *SGL* 2:98 "to converse (confidentially)";
with comitative, 56.

addaₓ-kú (addaₓ = LÚ × BAD. Cf. *MSL*, 2:77:626; Reiner, Šurpu 66);
written LÚ-*šessig*, 127 (=dìm) "to devour corpses." ur-gim R, 127. Cf.
SLTN 61:178 f.: ur-gu-la-gim addaₓ-kú-za nu-uš in-ga-zu-ám,
said of Ninurta; in a similar context, *Sumer*, *18*:21-35, we find dìm-ma
ug₄-ge-t[a]. Therefore, we should not exclude the possibility of reading
dìm-kú if the sign is LÚ-*šessig* or LÚ × GAM, as dìm also has the meaning
"dead"; cf. *JCS*, *19* (1965), 15, l. 68 and *VS* 2:12 ii 11–12 = *RA*, *8* (1911),
163, l. 27, where the meaning is certainly "dead" and the sign is LÚ-*gunû*
or LÚ × GAM. Parallels: WZJ 9:237:335: ᵍⁱˢal-zú-si-ga-ni muš
addaₓ-kú; *ZA*, *56* (1964), 84: ᵍⁱˢtukul ušumgal-gim addaₓ-kú(-e) =
kakku ša kīma ušumgalli šalamta ikkalu; ibid.: ur addaₓ-kú-gim.

addaₓ(LÚ × BAD) = var. of lú-éše, 50. Probably stands for LÚ × GÁNA-
tenû.

aga-zi(d): *agû kēnu* "right crown." Cf. Römer, *SKIZ* 215, 257, and the
relief of Enheduanna (see frontispiece) on which she is wearing this tiara.
R-dè ki-ága, "loving the R," 4; R-nam-en-na, 107. Cf. Sjöberg,
Nanna, p. 104, l. 8 nam-en-na šu-du₇-a R gùr-ru-me-en = *be-lu-
tam šu-uk-lu-lu a-ga-am ki-na-am na-šu-ú*; cf. also *SGL*, 1:97.

a-gim: *kî*, *kī'am*, "how!" "in that way," 115, 147.

aka: auxiliary verb "to do, make." See ki-su-ub . . . R, 116.

ama: *ummu*, "mother," 97, 149.

ama-ugu: *ummu alittu*, "natural mother." R-ni-ir diri-ga, 61; cf. van Dijk, *Bi Or, 11* (1954), 87, n. 40: mí-šul-la ama-ni-ra diri-ga.

a-ma-ru (<a-gi₆-uru$_x$[EN]): *abūbu*; kur-a-ma-ru, "flood mountain," 78. R kur-bi-ta e₁₁-dè, 11; see kur-bi-ta below.

an: *šamû*; *anu* "heaven," "God of Heaven." *elû* (wr. mostly BÀD = an$_x$, un$_x$, or ù-na; cf. *Acta Or* 28:54 ad 15), 86 f.; R-gim mah-a, 123; R-pa/úr, 112, cf. *ZA, 37* (1927), 247; giš-ká-R-na, 150, see giš-ká below; sag-kal-R-ki-a, 12.

an-NE-ke₄, var.: an-NE-ke₄-eš "midday," in parallelism with gi₆-ù-na, 140. This may be the same expression as that which is read by Römer, *SKIZ*, 175 and 269, an-šeg₆-gá and cf. also *CAD,Ṣ*, 214b s.v. *ṣiru* = an-bir$_x$(NE). Note nevertheless that the third sign is not—at least not always—GÁ, but GÁN, and reading -gá is ruled out by our -ke₄. Cf. Kramer, *AS, 12* (1940), 86; Falkenstein, *ZA, 47* (1942), 192; *AnOr* 29:91; Sollberger, *AfO, 16* (1953), 326. The gloss in *AfO, 7* (1931–32), 273:2:29 an-NE^{bi-ir} could stand for an-bar (cf. Sjöberg, *Nanna*, p. 128) with a similar meaning. For different meanings of an-NE, cf. Weidner, *Bab, 6* (1912), 65 ff. Against a reading an-šeg₆-gá speaks also *Enm.* 159 f.: kin-gi₄-a gi₆-ù-na im-diš (cf. *CAD,I*, s.v. *ištānu* and *AfO, 19* [1959–60], 50, ll. 16 f.)-gim še₇-gá/an-NE.GÁN-k̄a im-du₈ (cf. *Acta Or* 28:55)-gim zi-ga, as the genitive + locative *ak-a remains unexplained and is in fact quite impossible. All the instances quoted by Römer, *SKIZ* 175 and 269, fit a reading GÁN better. As the var. guarantees the reading ke₄, we abstain from any suggestion for the reading of GÁN. For the meaning, cf. Weidner, *Bab*, ibid.; *AHw*, s.v. *kararû* and for ref. Römer, *SKIZ*.

an-uraš: *šamû u erṣetu*; *anu u antu*; cf. Falkenstein, *ZA, 52* (1957), 72 ff.; Sjöberg, *Nanna*, pp. 67, 79, n. 14; ki-ága-R-a, 2.

a-nir: *tānīhu* "dirge." balag-R-ra, 33: R-ki-gar-ra, 97; ^{giš}má-R-ra, 98; see é-R-gal-gal-la, 25.

^{d}a-nun-na: *anunnakkū*, cf. Falkenstein-Kienast, *AS, 16* (1965), 127 ff.; 113, 116; R-dingir-gal-gal-e-ne, 34, 115.

a-ra-zu: *teslītu* "prayer," R . . . du₁₁, 81.

asila^{la} (var. -lá; si-il-li, cf. Gud. Cyl. A 19:1–2: si₁₆-lí-a . . . u₄ . . . zal): *rēšātu* "rejoicing, acclaim." R . . . du₁₁, 68.

aša: *ēdu* "alone." R mah-me-en, 134.

^{d}aš-ím-babbar; cf. Sjöberg, *Nanna*, p. 149, n. 2; 84, 102; see ^{d}nanna, ^{d}su'en.

ba: *zāzu* "distribute." See me-ba below.

bad (phon. /dr/): *nesû* "remove." ki-za R-rá-dè, var. of ba-e-dè-sù-dè, 43.

ba-da-ra: see gíri-R below.

bala: *nabalkutu*. See ki-R below.

balag: *balaggu* "harp." Cf. *CAD,B*, s.v.; R-a-nir-ra, 33.

ba(r): *naprušu* "fly, flee." Cf. *AS*, *16* (1965), 135, n. 112; du$_6$-dè mu-e-ši-ba-ra-aš, var. -íb-ra-aš, 35.

billuda: *pilludû*, "rite, ordinance," often written pi-lu$_5$-da. Cf. *AnOr* 28:29; Deimel, *Or.*, O.S. 2:16 f.; *SLTN* 80:6: R-nam-lugal-la; logogr.: PA.AN, but read billuda and cf. the var. PA.AN-da; R-gal-gal, 16; cf. *PBS* 13:40:2: pi-lu$_5$-da-gal-gal.

búr: *šuparruru*; *pašāru* "loosen"; "reveal, interpret." Cf. the frequent gada-gim búr "to loosen like a linen garment," e.g.: *SLTN* 49:3: gada-gim im-mi-in-búr; note the syllabic spelling in *CT* 42:36:7: gada-gim bí-in-bur. nì-kù-šà-ga-na . . . R, 57; du$_{11}$-du$_{11}$-ga . . . R, 119.

dab$_5$: *ṣabātu* "seize, capture." 91.

dagal: *rapāšu* "broad." ki-gim R-la, 124.

dal: *naprušu* "fly." im-mi-in-R, 18; R-a, 35; ba-ra-an-R-e(n), 105; see dé-dal below.

dalla-è: *šūpû* "appear, shine." *ZA*, *49* (1949), 129 and 26; u$_4$-R, 1.

dam: *mūtu/aššatu* "spouse." *NG 3*, s.v.; 55; R-díb-ba, 141.

dé: weak form of túm: *abālu* "carry," "increase (e.g. the flood)." úš ma-ra-an-R, 45, var. -túm; var. of túm/du$_{11}$, 72.

dè-dal: *ditallu* "ashes." For dè-dal as a noun, cf. Salonen, *JEOL* 18:334 f. and *CAD,D*, s.v. ditallu (since the Sum. dè-dal should be nominalized, one expects ditallû); as a verb: dè mu-ni-in-dal, 44.

di: *dīnu* "sentence, judgment." *NG 3*, 96; di-ní-gá, 117.

di-du$_{11}$: "prosecute a claim in court"; "render a verdict." *NG 1*, 9, n. 6; *NG 3*, s.v.; cf. *NG 1*, ibid.: ensí-ke$_4$ . . . di in-na-an-du$_{11}$; the two meanings suit the context in 102: di . . . ba-ra-bí-du$_{11}$, but "plead in favor of" may fit better than "render a verdict," as the context states that Su'en's influence is not strong enough (bí-in-du$_{11}$ nam-mu). Cf. also *BIN* 8:154:40: di íb-da-du$_{11}$; ibid. 155:17, 157:14: di-bi di hé-bé.

di-kúr: *dīnu šanû* "alien, hostile judgment." Cf. Ebeling, *Handerhebung*, 40:6 = *KAR* 58 rev. 7; cf. also *NG 3*, s.v. kúr; di-kúr di-mu-gim, 117. Cf. *ZA*, *57* (1965), 56, l. 128 kur-kur-re di-di-bi ba-kúr; Falkenstein reads silim-silim-bi etc., but cf. *BiOr*, *23* (1966), 243, l. 11: mí-zi eš-bar-du$_{10}$-kalam-ma-kam di-di-bi gal-zu; di-di-bi ba-kúr, *ZA*, ibid., could well be translated *alaktašu šanāt*; cf. *CAD,A*, s.v. *alaktu*.

di-til "render a definitive verdict." *NG 3*, 99 f.; cf. *ditillû*, *dīnu gamru*; di-ní-gá nu-mu-un-til, 117; cf. also comment ad loc. (above, p. 59, n. 57).

díb: *kamû* "fetter"; *ṣabātu* "capture." dam-R-ba (*ša ikkamû*), 141.

dingir: *ilu/iltu* "deity." R-gal-gal, 34, 115; R-zi, 64 = *ilu kēnu*, opp.: *ilu lemnu*.

diri: *atāru* "be great," "surpass." With dat. or loc.: "greater than." Cf. *SGL* 2:51; with dat.: 59, 61, 115; with loc.: 42. See ama-ugu; im-ma-si; kur-ra- R-ga. "To be greater than An" is said of several gods: (^{d}en-ki) an-ra R-ga, NBC 7806; (^{d}nergal) an-ra R-ga, *SGL*, 2:36; (^{d}inanna) an-^{d}en-líl-da(-ar) R-ga, innin-šà-gur$_4$-ru, *Belleten, 16* (1952), 354, Pl. 65 iii 22 (cf. van Dijk, *Acta Or* 28:15, n. 28); (^{d}nanna) lugal-nam-nam-ma an-ra R-ga, NBC 5452:26.

du: var. of gá (=weak form of gin), 106.

dù: var. of tu-ud, 138; see above, Chapter 5, n. 71.

du$_6$: *nigiṣṣu* "cleft, cave," 35; var.: du$_{10}$; di. Cf. Falkenstein, *AS, 16* (1965), 136, n. 139.

du$_7$: 1. *asāmu* "fit." 2. (phon. /dr/) *nakāpu* "gore." 1.: a-ra-ab-du$_7$, var. du$_{11}$, 108. 2.: u$_4$-R-R-gim í-R-R-dè, 28.

du$_8$ (duh/r, weak form da): 1. *paṭāru* "free." 2. *ulluhu* "clothe." 1.: ha-ba-du$_8$-e(n), 75; mu-e/un-du$_8$-e(n), 76. Cf. for this form the remark of D. O. Edzard, *ZDMG, 109* (1959), 239 f., n. 12a: the form must be translated "(An) *will* free me"; there are more forms supporting the opinion of Edzard. 2.: hi-li-ma-az... R-R, var. sù-sù, 146.

du$_{10}$: *damāqu*; *ṭābu* "be good, sweet." me-R-ga, 1; kaš-R-ga, 82; u$_4$ ba-an-na-R, 146; var. of du$_6$, 35.

du$_{11}$: 1. *qabû*; *zamāru* (cf. asila... du$_{11}$ etc.) "speak, sing" = *hamṭu*; enclitic: -di; di-di and e: *dabābu* = *marû*. 2. Auxiliary verb: "make." Cf. Langdon, *Bab, 7* (1923), 83 and Thureau-Dangin, *ZA, 17* (1903), 198, n. 1. inim-R-R, 15; kur za-ra... R, 51; inim-kù... R, 53; šír-kù... R, 63; gal-bi-R, 64; me-zu... R, 65; asila... R, 68; a-da-lam... R-mu-na-ab, 76; bí-in-R, 103; ma-ab-R, 108; R-R-ga, 119; za-a-kam... R, 122, 133; hé-zu-hé-za$_x$... R, 122, 133; mir-mir... R, 135; nì... ma-ra-an-du$_{11}$-ga, 139; du$_{11}$-ga-ni, 151. Var. of tu-ud, 138; of túm, 72; of du$_7$, 108; of du$_{10}$, 146; of e, 76, 83. See s.vv. di-R; silim-ma... R; sá-R; i-lu... du$_{11}$/e; see e.

du$_x$(DUN): var. of du/gá, q.v.

dub: *šapāku* "pour out, pile up." izi-ur$_5$... R, 136.

dúb: see á-R above.

dul: *katāmu* "cover." See u$_x$-lu-da... R below.

dumu: *māru*; *mārtu* "son, daughter," 96, 141.

dumu-gal: *mārtu rabītu* "eldest (son,) daughter." R-^{d}su'en-na, 41, 58. Cf. in-nin ša-gur$_4$-ra 2 = *Sumer, 13* (1957), 69, ll. 4 f. dumu-gal-^{d}su'en-na = dumu-mí ^{d}su'en *rabītum*.

durud(KÚ): see KA.KA-durud below.

e: *dabābu* "speak." *marû* of du$_{11}$ q.v.; a-a-ugu-za li-bí-in-eš, 52; a-da-lam ba-an-na-ab-bé-en, var. du$_{11}$, 76; ša$_6$-ga na-an-da-ab-bé, 55. Var. of du$_{11}$, 83; see i-lu... du$_{11}$/e.

é: *bītu* "house." é-bi, 88, 89; é-ta... è, 104. See éš-dam below.

é-a-nir-ra: *šubat tānihti*, King, *Magic*, 15:15, "house of mourning." R-gal-gal-la, 25 = euphemism for the netherworld; cf. *HAV* 10:15 (=hymn to Nungal) + dupl.: gìri mu-un-díb R-šè.

é-an-na: *ajakku* "sanctuary," 86.

è: *aṣû*; *šūpû* "emerge, appear." iti$_x$ . . . -R, 147. Var. of e$_{11}$, 104; see dalla-R, 1; gú-R, 153; u$_6$ zi-dè-eš . . . R, 148.

e$_{11}$: *elû*; *arādu*; *itellû* "ascend, descend, remove." é-ta . . . R, var. è, 104; kur-bi-ta R, var. è$^?$, 11.

en: *ēnu*; *ēntu* "high priest(ess)," 67, 120, 131. See nam-R below.

en-hé-du$_7$-an-na: 67, 81.

^{d}en-líl: 18, 95.

en-na: see še-ga.

èn-tar: *paqādu*; *šitūlu* "take care of." èn-mu ba-ra-bí-in-tar, 100; for the syntax cf. *PBS* 10/4:1:1:14 = *SRT* 40:3: en-na-me-šè (*adi mati*) dingir ga-ša-an-bé èn-bi nu-tar-re.

èš-dam: *aštammu*; epithet of a temple of Inanna; later "brothel." Cf. *AHw*, s.v.; *OECT* 1:15:3:7 ff. + parallels (cf. *Acta Or* 28/1:4) and *ZA*, *56* (1964), 118 f.; é-èš-dam-kù "the holy *aštammu*," 137.

^{d}ezinu: Ašnan; "grain," 10, 43.

gá: weak form of gin (*hamṭu*); bí-in-R-e(n) "he made me go to . . ."; var. du; du$_x$(DUN), 106.

gá-gá: doubled weak form of gar (*marû*). See sag-R below. Cf. ^{gá}gar, var. of gál, 137. (gá is here the simple weak form = *hamṭu*.)

gaba-tab: "clasp to the breast." Cf. refs. Römer, *SKIZ* 254 f.; me-R, 8.

gal: *rabû* "great." dumu-R, 41, 58; ká-R, 44; nin-R, 60; gal-gal: billuda-R, 16; me-R, 6; suh-kešda-R, 3; a-nir-R, 25; dingir-R, 34, 115.

gal-bi: *rabîš* "greatly." *SBH* 2:64; Poebel, *GSG*, § 395; R-du$_{11}$, 64; cf. *CT* 36:26:9: gal bí-du$_{11}$ šà-ga-ni i$_7$-mah a-na-àm du-a-bi(šà . . . túm, cf. *bibil libbi*); *SGL* 1:12:18: R du$_{11}$-ga-bé u$_4$ la-ba-ni-ib-sù-ud-dè; Reiner, *Šurpu*, 9:5: [nì]-ù-tu-ud-da úr-bi gaz R du$_{11}$-ga; *CT* 36:39:8: ^{d}nin-gír-su R mu-na-an-du$_{11}$; cf. also R . . . lu, R . . . gál, CT 36:42:6; R . . . túm, *ZA*, *51* (1955), 79, l. 155; R . . . gin, *ZA*, *52* (1957), 17, l. 19.

gal-zu: *eršu* "wise, omniscient." (fixed form from gal-an-zu); R igi-gál: *eršu u mudû*, 62; cf. YBC 13523:II: (^{d}nisaba) gal-zu igi-gál-dingir-re-e-ne.

gál: *bašû* "be, exist." ma-ra-R (*bašû* + dat.), 137; la-ba-ši-R, var. gub, 10; for gál + term., cf. refs. Römer, *SKIZ* 36:83 (S and 3 new duplicates; cf. *BiOr*, *23* [1966], 246) and 124:62; *CT* 36:39:25: lugal-šè húl-la hu (var. ša)-mu-un-ši-ni-ib-gala$_7$; ibid., 41:2: lugal-šè šu-mu-un-ši-íb-gala$_7$; ibid., 36:40:3; 36:39:26; 36:40:3. See nir-R; i-lu-ér-ra-ke$_4$-R; hul-R; zi-R; and zi-šà-R below.

gala: *kalû* "ritual singer," 140.

gar: *šakānu* "put." bí-in-R, 69; var. of gál, 10; weak form: gá, cf. ^{gá}gar, var. of gál, 137. See sag-gá-gá and ki-R below.

gi: var. of gi$_4$: 10, 30, 53, 56, 73, 88, 110, 140, 145.

gi$_4$: *târu*; *turru* "(re)turn." ka-gìri-za... R, 53; sahar-ta... R, 73; la-la ba-ra-... R, 88. See sig$_x$-R below.

gig: See hul-R below.

gin: *alāku* "go." mu-re-R, 22 (var. du$_{11}$, read du?), 25; cf. gá above (weak form).

gi$_6$-pár: *gipāru*, cf. *CAD,G*, s.v.; R-kù, 66.

GÍR, var. giš-R, giš-ú-R, giš-R^{ha-ah}, giš-R^{ah}; ki-R-kur-ra, 106. Several readings are possible: 106 reads ki-GÍR-kur-ra with var.: GÍR^{ha-ah} and GÍR^{ah}. 1. A reading šeg$_x$ is possible, cf. *VS* 2:2 ii 36 tu^{mušen} ne-te-a ù-še-eg-e bí-lá with *RA*, *8* (1911), 166:69 tu^{mušen}? ní-te-ni ^{giš}ú-GÍR-e bí-in-[lá]. This gives the Sumerian reading Akkadian *ašāgu*, which is a "loan" from Sumerian: ù-še-eg is to *ašāgu* as ù-šuh$_5$ is to *ašūhu*. Cf. M. Held, *AS*, *16* (1965), 396 f. 2. The gloss ha-ah gives a reading hah$_x$ = GÍR. Cf. Thompson, *DAB* 178 = *puquttu* "thistle," which fits the context well. The same is found in *TMH nF* 3:36:62 = *SRT* 4:55. 3. Thus the var. GÍR^{ah} has to be compared with the preceding and not with *MSL* 5:134:441 f.: ^{giš}GÍR.HAR. Cf. *CAD,E*, s.v. *eddetu*; *AHw*, s.v. *ašāgu* and *eṭṭettu*. Falkenstein, *ZA*, *57* (1965), 122 f. quoting *AS*, *12* (1940), 62, l. 368: har-ra-an ^{giš}gigir-e ba-ab-gar-ra-za ^{giš}AD-kur-ra ba-mú; cf. Lugalbanda and Anzu 270 (= *SEM*, 1 + *OECT* I 5 + *SEM*, 6): (i.e. *eṭṭettu*) ^{giš}ú-šeg$_x$-kur-ra, var. ^{giš}GÍR-kur-ra.

gíri-ba-da-ra: *paṭru u patarru* "dagger and sword." R ma-an-sì, 108. Mentioned in connection with *kurgarrû*; for refs. cf. Römer, *SKIZ* 130 f.: 72–75 and ibid., 165 f. Note that in the catalogue of me's in Inanna and Enki (e.g. *PBS* 5:25 rev. 21 f.), gíri-ba-da-ra follows immediately after kur-gar-ra; cf. also Gössmann, *Era-Epos*, 4:55–58.

gìri: *šēpu* "foot." R-ni-šè... ná, 78.

gìri(-a/e)... si: "put between the legs"; "fill the legs." For si with loc./loc.-term., cf. Edzard, *ZA*, *53* (1959), 12–15. gìri-za nu-kúš-ù i-in-si, 32; nu-kùš-ù, q.v., is here the subject. Cf. *BRM* 4:9:37: giš-gù-di me-ri-a-né i-im-si; *SLTN* 61:41 f. = 56 f.: ^{d}šakan lugal-anše-ke$_4$ gìri-za im-mi-in-si. Cf. also the familiar expression šu-(mah-)e/a... si, e.g. *HAV* 10:23 + dupl.; *ZA*, *52* (1957), 74 ad 32; = *ina qātē* x *mullû* / *ina šēpē* x *mullû*.

gìri-zé-er: *neḫelṣû* "remove the feet, withdraw." Cf. *CAD,I*, 235d.; šà-tùr-bi-ta R, 54; Heidel, *AS*, *13* (1940), 73: iz-zi dal-ba-an-na úr-bi ba-an-zé-er: *i-gar bi-ri-ti i-ši-iš-su it-te-hi-il-ṣu*; for zé-er "remove from," cf. *JCS*, *5* (1950–51), 6, l. 127 túg-šu-gur-ru... lú ba-da-an-zé-er. Is this the same root as zé-er: *pasāsu*? Cf. *TLB*

2:17:12–17: lú a-gú-bi su-^{d}na-na-a-ta íb-ta-an-zi-zi-a šà-zi-ke$_4$-éš ù in-gá-gá-a ù íb-zé-re-a (=*pasāsu*). Cf. refs. in Römer, *SKIZ* 113; the root of íb-ta-an-zi-zi seems to be the same as ba-da-an-zé-er, but is not easily explainable as the doubled weak form of zé-er, this being *marû*. Does *marû* also mean intensive?

gi-rin. See giš-ná-gi-rin, below.

giš-ká(n): *giškanakku* "doorsill." giš-ká-an-na-ke$_4$ silim-ma mu-na-ab-bé, var. om. -an-, 150. *giš-ká(n)-ak is a syntactical compound often written giš-ká-an-na. Cf. Gud. Cyl. A xxi:13–16: giš-ká-na im-gá-gá-ne an-si$_x$(NISIG$_x$ = SAR; cf. *CAD,B*, 93d and an-sig$_7$)-ga men íl-la-àm giš-ka-na-ta ba-ta-díb é-mah an-da gú-lá-àm; Gud. Cyl. A xxv:7–9 ^{giš}ti ká-e ús-sa-bi nir-an-na an-né ús-sa-àm giš-ká-an-na-bi é-ninnu u$_4$-ka-ba gù-di tés-ba gub-ba-àm (cf. van Buren, *Or. NS*, *13* (1944), 281–87); *ZA*, *57* (1965), 56, l. 124: giš-ká-na-bi ba-ra-an-si-ig; *SBH* 80:20 = 92b:27 + dupl.: giš-ká-an-na (var. om. -an-)-bi ba-ra-an-si-il. These instances show that giš-ká-an-na often varied with giš-ká-na. Nevertheless, giš-ká-an-na-ke$_4$, var. -ka, seems to mean here "doorsill to Heaven," for Su'en evidently appears as the new moon in heaven. Cf. also si-gar-an-na; ig-an-na, etc. For the contraction, cf. ga-ša-an-an-na < ka-ša-na. If the author meant that Su'en came to the *gipāru*, beautiful like the new moon, then the same meaning as giš-ká-an-na in the Gudea quotations can be accepted. Cf. also Salonen, *Türen*, p. 54; Radau, *HAV* 400; Römer, *SKIZ* 224, 234 f.; Falkenstein, *ZA*, *57* (1965), 98 ad 124.

giš-ná, eme-sal: mu-ná: *eršu* "bed." giš-ná-gi-(var.: gi$_4$)-rin-na, 118. For the adjective girin, cf. Falkenstein, *ZA*, *52* (1957), 59, l. 18 and the refs. ibid., 68 f.; Sjöberg, *Nanna*, p. 162: gu-za-gi-rin; gug-gi-rin. girin has perhaps a wider range of meanings converging in "blossoming, fruitful, shining." Cf. *unnubu*. Cf. also Hallo, *BiOr*, *20* (1963), 140 f. girin is the result of adorning the bed with herbs and perhaps flowers. Cf. *TRS*:70:40 f.: giš-ná-gi$_4$-rin-na . . . gub . . . ú-za-gìn-dur$_5$-ru [m]u-ne-da-ab-pàra-ge-ne (cf. Castellino, *ZA*, *52* [1957], 52); *Enm.* 562: R-še-er-kán-di$_9$(dug$_4$, enclitic weak form; therefore -ga is lacking) šu li-bí-in-dag R-gi-rin-na la-ba-an-du$_{11}$. The attribute is mostly used of the ritual couch in the Dumuzi-Inanna cult: Kramer, *PAPhS*, *107* (1963), 503, l. 50: mu-lu-bé é-šà-ga mu-ná-gi-rin dè-bí-in-aka; ibid., p. 495, l. 40: R-na-mu ùku na-ab-gub-bu-ne, etc. Cf. Kramer, *AS*, *10* (1938), 38, 80.

gi$_6$-ù-na (gi$_6$-un$_x$(BÀD)-na, cf. Gud. Cyl. A xi 26 gi$_6$-a-na = gi$_6$-an-na): *mūšu* "(mid)night," 56, 139. Frequently in parallelism with an-NE.GÀN, q.v.; cf. refs. in Römer, *SKIZ* 175.

gizzu (from giš-zu$_x$(MI), cf. an-zu$_x$^{mušen} and the var. giš-zu$_x$-dè . . . te): *ṣillu* "shadow, shade," 71.

[gú: *kišādu*]
gú-è: *halāpu* "wrap." hi-li R, 153.
gú-en-na: (*gu'ennakku*), "throne room." Explained by *nap-har be-lí*, "assemblage of lords," in Lugal-e I 24 (Kinnier Wilson, *ZA*, *54* [1963], 72; cf. also *KAR* 18:6 f.); nir-gál-R-ke$_4$, 143.
gú-giš-gar: "submit." *AnOr* 28:127; ^{d}a-nun-na-ke$_4$-ne R, 113.
gú-tuku: *ašarēdu* "first, foremost." Falkenstein, *ZA*, *55* (1963), 48; nin R, 143.
[gù: *rigmu*]
gù-dé (from gù-du$_{11}$, weak form): *ragāmu* "roar." kur-ra R, 125a.
gù-ra-ra: *ragāmu*; *šasû* "roar, shout." *LSS*, *NF* 1:83:7 f.; *CT* 16:30:53 f.; *RA*, *18* (1921), 38, l. 6; *SGL*, 2:43; u$_4$ R-ta gù im-da-ab-ra-ra (comitative; identifies Inanna with the storm), 29.
gub: with terminative: "do service." *NG*, *2*, 96 ad 58; á-ága-an(a)-ke$_4$ R, 19; var. of gál + term., 10. See ù-ma-R, 104, 132.
gub-ba: in gub-ba-šà-ga-na, 80, is not imperative and cannot be *kūn libbi* in the favorable sense of this expression, but stands for the more common íb-ba-šà-ga-na in this text. Cf. perhaps lú-gub-ba: *mahhû* "ecstatic." The meaning "stubbornness" would fit the context well. Perhaps: "haughtiness."
gu-ul: *rabû*/*šurbû* "be great, exalted," 134, 142.
gul-gul: *abātu*; *ubbutu* "destroy, devastate." kur-R, 17; ki-lul-la hé-R-e, 101; ki-bala R, 125.
gúr(um/un): *kanāšu* "bend, bow down." kur R-R, 20. Cf. for the reading: Kramer, *JCS*, *18* (1964), 46, n. 89: [é-zi-mu$^?$ mu-u]n-GAM^{gu-ru}; *STVC* 65:2:2 [dingir-ki-a] mu-⌜na⌝-ku-ru-ne-[eš], var. for mu-na-gúr(un)-e-eš in Lipit-Ištar *25, Römer, *SKIZ* 12:24; *SLTN* 103:12 = Krecher, *ZA*, *57* (1965), 30: é-a-ni gúr(um)-ma-ni mu-di-di-in; *TRS* 81:7 = van Dijk, *MIO*, *12* (1966), p. 70: šibir kur-kur-ra guru-ma! Note ^{giš}GAM = ^{giš}guru$_5$(-uš) = *ku(r)ṣim(t)u*, *MSL*, 6:23:212 and note; also giguru = *gigurû* "slanted reed," contra *CAD,G*, 70c.
guruš: *eṭlu* "(young) man." R-á-tuku, 48. R-šà-gan "adults," cf. *CAD,G*, s.v. *gitmālu*; for šà-gan cf. ama-gan/gán > ugu(n) = *ālidu*, *alittu*.
hé-zu-hé-za$_x$ (ZU; var. -za): fixed verbal form; cf. perhaps *CAD,I*, s.v. *idûtu*, "knowledge," which has as Sumerogram: x a-da-min and [x]-zu-a. Cf. the comments on line 122 and below s.v. za-a-kam. For the vowel-alternation, cf. below s.v. i-lu-lam-ma and *Acta Or* 28^1:39, n. 100. This vowel-alternation is used in Sumerian to express reciprocity: "to and fro," "hin und wieder"; the alternation can be u-a, as in one part of the manuscripts, or a-u, as in the other part. The vowel-alternation can be u-e, cf. *CT* 15:14:36: a-KAL x̣-zu nu-uš bí-in-tuk bar-zu né-eš mi-ni-gál and see *TLB* 2:6:3:4 ff.: ú-ru a-še-er-ra ni-iš bi-gu-la.

Cf. also the articles of Emeneau on "echo-words" in Dravidian Tamil, *JAOS*, *58* (1938), 553; *59* (1939), 503.

hi-li: *kuzbu* "beauty." Römer, *SKIZ* 175; R gú-è, 153; R ba-ra-mu-un-til, 88.

hi-li-ma-az: "joyous beauty." Cf. *SGL* 2:42: R-za-na = *el-ṣi-iš kun-zu-bu*, *CAD,E*, 109d; 146, with var. ma-ra-az.

hul (cf. gul) *šulputu*; *ubbutu* "destroy." R-a . . . ku₄, 89. See ku₄.

hul-gál: *lemnu*; *lemēnu*; *lemniš* "wicked, (act) wickedly." šà-R, 39.

hul-gig: *zêru*; *zīru* "hate, hated, hostile." ki-bala-R, 93.

húl: *rēšu* "rejoice." šà ì-R, 40 (possessive complex).

hur-sag: *šadû* "mountain," 43.

huš: *ezzu* "fierce, terrible." See igi-R, 36, 128; me-R, 23; nì-me-gar-R, 22; sag-ki-R, 37.

i₇: *nāru* "river," 45.

i-lu: *qubû* "cry" (<i-lum, cf. *AS*, *12* (1940), 26, l. 87 i-lu-ma si-ga; with vowel-alternation lum-ma-lam-ma q.v. and cf. *CT* 19:41 K4328:1:19a–b i-lu-a-li = *lallaru*). i-lu-ír-ra-ke₄-gala₇, 24; for the genitive, cf. i-lu-šìr-ra = *nu-be-e ṣir-hi*, *CAD,Ṣ*, s.v.; R-hé-gál-la-kam, *JNES*, *23* (1964), 4, l. 43 and *CT* 15:26:1–21, Falkenstein, *ZA*, *47* (1942), 197. The expression is an expansion of ír-gig mu-un-ma-al = *mar-ṣi-iš i-bak-ki*, *SBH* 101:51. Cf. ibid. 94:23:39; 102:41; the construction with locative-terminative is apparently preserved in compound verbs like: a-nir gál; hul-gál etc.; cf. also s.v. ír-še₈-še₈.

i-lu . . . du₁₁/e: *ṣarāhu*; *qubê qabû*, *CAD,Ṣ*, s.v.; "sing a dirge," 24, 33. Cf. Römer, *SKIZ* 21:11 ff., with var. from YBC 4609: sipa-zi lú-i-lu-du₁₀-ga-ke₄ ur₅-ša₄(-àm) ša-(mu-)ra-ni-ib-bé, *BiOr*, *23* (1966), 244 f.

íb: *ezēzu*; *ezzu* "(be) angry." íb-ba, 41, 142; šà-íb-ba, 38.

[igi: *īnu* "eye"; *panū* "front"; *pān/mahar* "before."]

igi-šè . . . gin: "precede, come forward," Hallo, *JAOS*, *83* (1963), 174. Var. of ù-mu-re-gin, 22.

igi-gál: *igigallû*, *mūdû* "wise," 62. See gal-zu.

igi-gùn-gùn: *šit'āru*, "flashing eyes" Falkenstein, *ZA*, *44* (1938), 4–7; 130.

igi-huš: *ša panī ezzu*, *CAD,E*, 427a; 36; 128; R-íl-íl, 129: *ezziš nekelmû*, *CAD,I*, 155b.

igi-mè(*-ak): "before the battle"; as a noun "vanguard," 26. Cf. Kramer, *PAPhS*, *107* (1963), 503, l. 25 i-bi-mè-ka gub-ba-mu-dè (var. di-da-mu-dè) and *JCS*, *19* (1965), 17 for the parallelism with ka-mè; múru-mè, zum (var. zíb)-mè and egir-mè. ka-mè is there a noun, like igi-mè in our text.

igi-X-ak-a nigin: 117. The construction of this complex is different from igi-nigin = *ṣûd panī*, *CAD,Ṣ*, 228c; *suhhur panī*, Lambert, *AfO*, *18* (1957–58), 295 and Gadd, *Driver AV* 62:4: šà nu-si-si igi-nigin-bi uru^{ki}-ta ba-da-díb; igi-gá...nigin = *sahāru ina panija*; this expression is more descriptive than igi-gá...gál *bašû ina panija*; for nigin, cf. *AfO*, *16* (1952–53), 297, l. 12: ugu-lú-tu-ra-ke$_4$ mu-un-nigin, "(Asalluhi) moved over and around the sick man." Cf. also Landsberger, *WO*, *3* (1964), 51, n. 26.

íl: *našû* "lift, carry." me...R, 7; igi-huš R-R, 129.

im-hul: *imhullu* "evil wind." R-R, 31.

imin: *sebûm*; *kiššatu* "seven, 'all'." me-R-bi, 5.

im-ma-si-im-ma-diri-ga: fixed deverbal form; the meaning of si is found also in the fixed form íb-si. Cf. Bergmann, *ZA*, *57* (1965), 39 ad ši-mu *PBS* 10/2:3:rev. 5; diri means "it is too much"; from this meaning diri-ga = *ašuštu* seems to derive. They are the screams of suffering men or, as in 138, of women in travail. Cf. *Sagesse*, 15:14: R-ta zi al-ir-ir-re; *TRS* 57:19: im-ma-an-si-im-ma-diri-ga-ta. Cf. Witzel, *Or.*, *13* (1944), 298 l. 23 = Edubba-essay No. 2, for which cf. Gordon, *BiOr*, *17* (1960), 143.

^{d}inanna: kù-R, 83; šà-R, 145; R zà-mí, 153; an-ki-a ^{d}inanna-bi-me-en, 12; for this construction, cf. *OECT* 1:36:15: ^{d}nisaba-bi-me-en; Römer, *SKIZ* 38 ii 14: ^{d}utu-bi hé-me-en.

inga-/iga-: "again," "equally," 79. Cf. Poebel, *GSG* § 403; Falkenstein, *ZA*, *48* (1944), 89 ff.; van Dijk, *Acta Or.* 28:52; Jacobsen, *AS*, *16* (1965), 37. inga- frequently resumes -gim. Cf. refs. Falkenstein, ibid., and Kramer, *PAPhS*, *107* (1963), 494, l. 11 (cf. ibid., 13): a-a-zu-gim in-ga-dím.

inim-du$_{11}$-du$_{11}$: "make decisions," 15.

inim-kù: "the pure word," 15, 53; opp.: inim-gig (cf." Curse of Agade," 171; 221). Cf. *TRS* 19:50 f.; *CT* 36:31:22; *TRS* 22:8; *CT* 36:40:13f.; *CT* 36:26:10; *CT* 42:28:1.

ír: *bikītu* "tears, crying." R-a...šu-bar, 82.

ír-pà: "burst into tears"; dumu-R-da, 96; cf. Falkenstein, *ZA*, *56* (1964), 127 f.

ír-še$_8$-še$_8$: see i-lu-ír-ra-ke$_4$-gál$_7$...še$_8$-še$_8$, 24. For the different expressions and modifications of the words for "to weep," cf. *CAD,B*, s.vv. *bakû* and *bikītu*; *CT* 42:1:45: edin-na ír-gig mu-un-še$_8$-še$_8$ = e-di-né ír mu-bi i-ši-še, *JCS*, *8* (1954), 82:1:7 = edin-na ír mu-bi i-[še$_8$-še$_8$], YBC 4659:4. (R. Kutscher, unpubl. Yale thesis, 97 f.)

^{d}iškur: 10, 30.

iti$_x$(U$_4$·^{d}NANNA): "moonlight, new moon," 147. Cf. Sjöberg, *Nanna*, pp. 18 f.; Römer, *SKIZ* 175.

izi-ne-ne(r): "fan the fire." R-ra "fanned fire," R-ra kalam-e šèg-gá, 13. Cf. *4R* 24:2:17ab (*CAD,I*, s.v. *išhilṣu*) la ne-ne-ra mu-un-š[èg] = *iš-hi-il-ṣa u nab-le* [*ušaznin?*]; *UET* 6:137:72: an-ne IM-šèg (var. AS 12:36:189: bar-šèg, for which cf. *Sagesse* 117 ad 15′) íl-íl-i izi mu-uh-ne-ne-re *JCS*, *1* (1947), 10, l. 40: limmu-kam-ma izi-ne-ne...; read perhaps in *SBH* 55 rev. 29 f.: ne-$^{ni!-ni!-ir}$-ne = *ina i-šá-a-tum na-pi-ih-tim* against *CAD,I*, 229b and copy. For the rain of fire, cf. *CAD,I*, and *CAD,H*, v.v. *išātu, hamāṭu*, and *hummuṭu*; *OECT* 6:38:7 f.: kur-kur nigin-na-zu izi mu-un-da-an-[šub] šè-mur-gim ba-dub = *ina nap-har ma-ta-ti-ki i-šá-tam id-di-ma ki-ma tùm-ri iš-pu-uk*; ne-ne probably stands for nir-nir like ne-ne for nígin-nígin (cf. *Acta Or.* 28:28, n. 72); cf. also nir-nir = *zukkû* "winnow." *CAD,Z*, s.v. *zakû*, lex. sect.; nir-mud-da = *idiptu edēpu*; du$_{10}$-nir "inseminate." *Acta Or.* 28:50; NUN × NUN = né-né-er, *MSL*, 2:62:395. For izi píl-píl-lá, ibid. and *SAI* 3135–37. nir-nir is perhaps the same root as gír-gír in nim-R-R-. Cf. *Acta Or.* 28:27, n. 68.

izi-ur$_5$(eme-sal: še-mur): "coal." R mu-un-dub, 136. Cf. Salonen, *JEOL* 18:337 f.; Meissner, *MAOG* 11/1–2:81; R-ra = *pi-it-tum* "banked fire." Oppenheim, *Or.*, *N.S.* 19:130 f.; Hallo, *BiOr*, *20* (1963), 142 [6]; *ana pi-it-tim* "for the firepan," Kingsbury, *HUCA, 34* (1963), 6, l. 37 and n. 25. Cf. izi-ur$_5$-dugud-bi i-ra-a-ri i-NE-bi ("its smoke") ba-gul, Gadd, *Driver AV* 64:43; Salonen, *BM* 3:107 f.

KA.KA-durud$_x$(KÚ): "eat; feed on; peck at (with the beak)," 27. Cf. *NG* 3:9 ad 120b:15.

ka-gìri: *padānu* "path." R-za hé-e b-gi$_4$, var. ki-gìri, 53. Cf. gìri-ús R si-si-te = *šu-te-šu-ur ki-ib¹-si-im ù pa-da-ni-im*, *Sumer, 11* (1955), Pl. VI, 4; Kramer, *PAPhS, 107* (1963), 503, l. 31: kur-kur-ra ka-me-ri ba-ni-in-ne(=nigin); *JNES, 23* (1964), 2, l. 5: ama$_5$?-a-né (sag-gi$_4$-a) R al-gi¹-ba-ab.

ka-kešda: *kiṣru* "regiment"; in parallelism with ugnim, 46 f. Cf. *AHw*, s.v. *kiṣru(m)*, 8: "Kerntruppe"; 8d "Einsatzeinheit (des stehenden Heeres)"; *RA, 12* (1915), 74, ll. 11 f. R-mè-a gi-ne-da-zu-dè = *ki-ṣir ta-ha-za ina kun-ni-ka*; YBC 7196, cf. Hallo, *BiOr, 23* (1966), 246, *SKIZ* 35:77 f.: ^{kuš}e-íb-ùr-igi-tab-ugnim-ma-me-en / ur-sag-igi-zala-ga ka-kešda-ge-na-me-en.

ka-làl: *pu-ú d[i-iš-pi]* (*CAD,D*, 161a) "honey mouth." Römer, *SKIZ* 23:15; ibid., 64, n. 196; but read 23:15 du$_{11}$ làl-gim du$_{10}$ mu du$_{11}$-ge du$_7$ ("word sweet like honey, name worthy of praise"); *SGL* 2:82:34: lugal R-dingir-re-e-ne ^{d}en-ki; ibid., 107 R-ama-na-mu and frequently in Inanna-Dumuzi texts.

ká-gal: *abullu* "gate," 44. See giš-ká. For a proposed reading abulla, cf. Sjöberg, *RA, 60* (1966), 91.

kal: see sag-R.

kal-kal: *šūquru* "precious." nin-R, 109.

kalam: *mātu* "(native) land," 13, 18.

kar: *ekēmu* "take away." an-da é-an-na... R, 86; aga-zi... R, 107; nam-lugal-an-né... R, 77.

kaš-du₁₀: "sweet drink." ír... R-ga-gim, 82.

kešda: syll.: ki-ši, VAT 8381:4 (see below, s.v. sum); YBC 4705 (dupl. *UET* 8:70): 16: sizkur-ra nidba-bi ì-kin-en nì-nam nu-mu-ne-kešda^{ik?-ši}; d = phon. /dr/; cf. var. keš^d-re, 3. See ka-R above and sag-R and suh-R below.

ki: 1. *erṣetu* "earth"; 2. *ašru/ašar* "place, where." 1.: R-gim dagal, 124; R(-e)... sig₁₄-gi₄, 10. See an-ki. 2.: 92, 106.

ki-ága: *rāmu* "love," 2, 4, 18, 109, 111, 121, 135.

ki-bala: *māt nukurti* "rebellious country." R-hul-gig, 93. Cf. *CT* 14:16:22: R-hul-gig-a-a-ugu-zu-šè a-ba za-e-gim te-ba; R-gul-gul-lu, 125.

ki-e-ne-di: *mēlultu* "(place of) dancing." Cf. refs. in Römer, *SKIZ* 173 f.; R-bé mir i-in-si, 49.

ki-gar: *šakānu* "place (on the ground), establish." a-nir R-ra, 97 (for: balag-a-nir-ra R). Cf. *AS*, *12* (1940), 26, l. 86: balag-ír-ra ki-(a) al-gar-ra.

ki-bé... gi₄: *ana ašrišu tāru/turru*, 110, 145. šà... R, 145, or šà R-gi₄ (var.: gi-gi), 110 (both intransitive), is a standard conclusion of prayers, both the earlier letter-prayers and the later ír-šà-hun-gá prayers which replaced them. Cf. above, note 78 to Chapter 5, and for the present Bergmann, *ZA*, *57* (1965), 42; Civil, *Studies Presented to Oppenheim*, p. 89; YBC 4620:56 = 8630:22 (letter to Enki): šà-dingir-mu ki-bé ha-ma-gi₄-gi₄; YBC 6458 rev. 9 f.: šà sul-gi lugal-mu ki-bé ha-ma-gi₄-gi₄; *BE* 31:7:44b: šà-lugal-mu...-ma-gi₄¹-e.

ki-gìri: "path" (53, var. for ka-gìri, q.v.).

ki-lul-la: *šagaštu* "place of murder." R-la... gul-gul, 101. Cf. *ZA*, *52* (1957), 17, l. 18: ki-lul-la ur-^dnammu dug-gaz-gim a-ba-ni-in-tag₄-aš ("after having left U. on the place of murder..."); ibid., 32: ùku ki-lul-la ba-ab-lah₄-a-zu; *UET* 6/1:58 rev. 14: a-ki-lul-la a-lù-a bí-íb-nag(a)-me-eš. Cf. Falkenstein, *BiOr*, *22* (1965), 282 and n. 25; ki-lul-la, PN, ibid., and Hallo, *HUCA*, *33* (1962), 33 (sub Šulgi 47).

ki-sì-ga: *kisigû*; *kispu*; R-edin-na: *kisip ṣēri*; R bí-in-gar, 69. ki-sì-ga does not always mean "offerings for the dead" or the place where such offerings were brought. The ki-sì-ga is often found in the desert and the ritual against illnesses was performed there. Cf. IM 10135 (van Dijk, *Heidelberger Studien zum Alten Orient*, 1967, 240 f.): x sìla ì-nun... a-tu₅-a R-edin-na... dumu-mí-lugal-la *i-nu-ma im-ra-ṣú*. It is clear that this was not a ritual for the dead; a list of objects needed in this ki-sì-ga is found in *CT* 45:99: *hi-ši-ih-ti* R-edin-na (cf. also *TCL* 1:7). The original meaning of ki-sì-ga seems to be "a hole in the earth" which served as a dwelling place. The key place for this meaning is *ZA*, *50* (1952), 70, ll. 92 f.: ukù-R-bi-a . . . mu-mu hé-em-mi-sa₄. ki-sì-ga seems to be a word for the temporary hut where rituals were performed and for the dwelling place of the ill who were quarantined outside the city. Cf. for refs. *AHw*, s.v. *kisiggû*; "Curse of Agade," 256, 265; *ZA*, *57* (1965), 63. We understand ki-sì-ga here as such a hut, where Enheduanna was sitting like a patient, banished from the city, while the dust storms gave her face a ghostlike aspect and her beauty was changed into mud, like a corpse.

ki . . . su-ub, *qaqqara našāqu*, *šukênu*, "kiss the ground, prostrate oneself," 116 (variant). ᵈa-nun-na-ke₄-e-ne ki-a mu-un-su-ub-su-ub = ᵈ*a-nun-na-ki qaq-qa-ru ú-na-šá-qu* (Sjöberg, *Nanna-Suen*, p. 168, l. 27; cf. Falkenstein, *AS*, *16* [1965], 136, n. 125). ki-a he-su-ub = *lu-u tuš-ki-na*; *ŠL* 2:461:283.

ki-su-ub . . . aka: *qaqqara našāqu*; *šukênu* "kiss the ground, make obeisance." ᵈa-nun-na . . . R, 116; cf. Kramer, *AS*, *10* (1938), 28; *SGL* 2:32; Kapp, *ZA*, *51* (1955), 79, ll. 110 f.: nundum-bi-a ki-su-ub a-ra-aka-ne; *SRT* 17 rev.ii:7: mu-mu-šè kir(i)₄ ki-su-ub ha-ba-aka-ne; said of the Anunna, cf. Falkenstein, *AS*, *16* (1965), 136b and 4R 9a:57–60 (=*OECT* 6:16); Sjöberg, *Nanna*, p. 168, l. 27; *ŠL* 461:283. See ki-za.

[ki-za: weak form of the preceding, "to kiss the ground"; "make obeisance"; cf. kir(i)₄(KA) ki-za, *SGL* 2:32 and ki-za-za, Landsberger, *ZA*, *29* (1915), 288; *JAOS*, *69* (1949–50), 214; *MAOG* 4:306; Meissner, *MAOG* 12:2:36 ad II 19 f. za is the weak form of su-ub and cf. za$_x$ as the reading of ZU in hé-zu-hé-za$_x$, q.v.; ki-za is found in Sargonic inscriptions, cf. *AfO*, *20* (1963), 38, l. 18; in the inscription of Enheduanna, *UET* 1:23:8 f.: [kir₄-k]i-za-za [ᵈen-líl-ra] etc. Cf. also Geid. Cyl. Bi 13 (Falkenstein, *RCA* 3:157a): kir(i)₄-ki-zu-zu.]

ki-za . . . túm/tum: "carry away homage"; "refuse obeisance," 42, 59. Cf. van Dijk *apud* Garelli, ed., *Gilg. et sa légende*, 72 ad *TLB* II 4:82 = *JCS*, *1* (1947), 20, l. 151: šu-šè mu-un-dib ki-za nam-ba-an-túm (var. -tùm,-tum₄). The meaning of this expression should be clarified (so against van Dijk) by the idiomatic use of túm, as the meaning of ki-za appears assured. Cf. "Curse of Agade" 70 (*ZA*, *57* [1965], 70) uruᵏⁱ inim-inim-ma-bi ᵈutu ba-an-túm: "Utu carried away . . ."; the same meaning in the idiom: me-da . . . túm = *ajiš ubbal*. Cf. *CAD,A*, s.v. *ajiš*; Gordon, *Sumerian Proverbs*, p. 387 s.v. me-da-túm and p. 41, and translate there "when wickedness exerts itself, where will the Sungod bring it off, i.e., how will he succeed?" Ibid., p. 214: dub-sar šà-dab₅-ba nu-un-zu-a inim-bala-e me-da hé-em-túm "if the scribe does

not know how to render the sense (cf. inim-dab₅ = awāta šūhuzu), what
will the interpreter make of it (how will he succeed)?"

ki-za...sù/bad: "make homage far from," 43.

kú: akālu "eat, consume." See zi-R, 105; adda$_x$-R, 127; KA.KA-durud$_x$,
27.

kù: ellu, "holy, pure." R-ᵈinanna, 83; inim-R, 15, 53; éš-dam-R, 137;
gi₆-pàr-R, 66; šà-R, 61, 110; šìr-R, 63, 99.

ku₄(r): 1. erēbu "enter"; 2. "turn into." 1. 66, 90. See tab-ku₄; 2. hul-a
hu-mu-di-ni-in-R, 89 (var.: -gur; cf. Falkenstein, BiOr, 22 [1965],
283 ad UET 6/1:79 rev. 15); YBC 4620:48 = 8630:15: ki-kukú-ga-mu
u₄-šè ù-mu-e-ni-ku₄ (var. mu-ni-in-gar), and cf. Kramer, Two
Elegies, 54:89; Enheduanna B 118: ni-in-ta mu-nu-uš-ra mu-nu-uš
ni-in-ta-ar-ra ku-ku-te ᵈinanna za-a-kam = zi-ka-ra-am a-na
si-ni-ìš-tim si-ni-ìš a-na zi-ka-ri-im-ma tu-ru-um ku-um-ma eštar, cf.
CAD,Z, s.v. zikaru; SRT 36:21: nitá munus-a munus nitá-a-bi
ku₄-ku₄ and cf. Römer, SKIZ 130 ad Iddin-Dagan *6:60, 63; ír a-nir
i-ᵈutu-di-bi nì-gig-ga hé-ni-ku₄, Cod. Lipit-Ištar, epil. 14 f.; TRS
59:10: ...húl-la mu-un-ku₄ i-ᵈutu-bi mu-un-è; PBS 10/4:1:iii:
7-9 = Edzard, ZZB (1957), p. 87: urú-bi urú-šub-ba im-ma-
ni-in-ku₄-ra-àm...urú-gál-la-bi nu-gál-la mi-ni-in-ku₄-
ra-àm.

kur: šadû; mātu "mountain, (foreign) land." R-ra uš$_x$-...sì, 9; R
gurum-gurum, 20; R-ra diri-ga, 42; R za-ra, 51; nin-R-R-ra, 62;
ki-šeg$_x$-R-ra, 106; R-ra gù-dé, 125a.

kur-a-ma-ru: šād abūbi "mountain of/and (?) flood," 78.

kur-bi-ta...è: "descend from its mountain," 11. Cf. Gud. Cyl. A ix 19:
má-gan me-luh-ha kur-bi-ta im-ma-ta-e₁₁-ne.

kur-gul-gul: mu'abbit šadî, epithet of Inanna, 17, 152; cf. 125; BE 30:1
ii 2:4; 9 ii 20; 12:4; SBH 132:31 and frequently: R ga-ša-an-é-an-
na-mèn; VS 2:40:42: [kur-gu]-ul-gu-ul ka-ša-an-é-[an-na];
ibid., 29:3: nin-mah R, cf. SGL, 1:102; kù-zu-mu nin ga-ša-an-
ᵈgir-gi-lu / R mu-gi₁₇-ib-ga-ša-an-na, CT 15:23-2 f. Cf. CAD,
A/1:41 f.

kúr: nakāru; nukkuru "(be) hostile, alien"; ki-R, 98; nì...R, 85; šanû,
see di-kúr, 117.

kur-ra diri-ga, "supreme over the lands," 42; (Inanna) mí-kur-ra-
diri⁈-˹ga˺-BI-mèn-na (CT 42:13:30; cf. Kramer, PAPhS, 107 [1963],
503, l. 30).

kúš: anāhu: šūnuhu; 31, 85; see nu-kúš-ù, 32.

la-la: lalû, "vigor, appeal"; R-bi ba-ra-mu-un-gi₄, 88; cf. Sjöberg,
Nanna, p. 174 but strike Enheduanna A 56 and add ZA, 57 (1965), 53
and 87; R...sù-sù / var. du₈-du₈, 146; R...gùr, 147.

lá. See šu-lá; šu-šè...LÁ.

lah₄(DU + DU): *šalālu*, "capture," 46.

lu: *rite'û*; *dešû*. See ukù-lu-a.

lú: *awīlu* "man," 119.

lú-éše: *kalû* "prisoner." R ma-ra-ab-sar-re-eš, 50. Cf. *JCS*, *19* (1965), 16 ad 151 and correct in l. 151 hu-mu-[sarⁱ-r]eⁱ-eš, sar (q.v.) having the meaning *kuššudu* / *ṭarādu*.

ᵈlú-gu-la, 87; read perhaps an-lú-gu-la, var. an-lugal-gu-la. ᵈlú-gu-la occurs in *TRS* 10:121 between manifestations of the "mother-goddess" Dingir-mah or Ninhursanga (ll. 112–20) and her consort Šulpae (ll. 122–25; cf. Falkenstein, *ZA*, *55* [1963], 21). In Tablet II of the canonical God-List, it occurs in the midst of the former as a manifestation of Belit-ili (Deimel, Pantheon, No. 1837), but this name hardly fits our context.

lú-uₓ-lu. See nam-R.

lù-lù: *dalāhu*. See mir-mir, 135.

lugal-an-né: King of Uruk. Cf. commentary, p. 56; the reading as a personal name seems imperative: no scribe would write -an-né for an-na, and Sîn is simply not *šar šamê*; 74, 77.

lul. See ki-lul-la.

lum-a-lam-ma. Cf. commentary ad ll. 122, 135. See i-lu; hé-zu-hé-zaₓ; doubled i-lu(m) with vowel-alternation; for the forms i-lu-lam-ma and e-lu-lam, cf. the references collected by Falkenstein, *ZA*, *56* (1964), 51 f. and add: *SEM* 58:4:33, colophon of the "Marriage of Martu": NI.NA.A[B.KI i-me]-a lum-a-lam-ma; *TRS* 70:34: mí-e nì-i-lu-lam-ma-na. Cf. perhaps Lugalbanda and Anzu 248 (*SEM*, 1 iv 16 = *SLTN* 2 rev. 10): ur-bar-ra-gim lum-lam mi-ni-i[b-z]a (="bark-ing"?); *TRS* 92:13 (ᵍⁱˢal 94): ᵍⁱˢal lum-lum-ma ᵍⁱˢal lam-lam-ma (+dupl.); *VS* 2:27:11 šeš i-bí-lum-lum-mu šeš i-bí-lá-lá-mu. Not relevant here: *JCS*, *16* (1962), 79:3625:22: šu-gìri ág-lum-ma-lam-ma-ni ì-li hé-em-luh-e and *TRS* 20:66: ba-lam ba-lam = *PAPhS*, *107* (1963), 508b, (based on N4305?) l. 1: ba-lum ba-lum-lum; this is certainly the verb *unnubu*/*uššubu*. Cf. now also Civil, *JCS*, *20* (1966), 119–21.

ᵍⁱˢmá: *elippu* "boat." R-a-nir-ra, 98. Lines 97–99 are very obscure; like lines 151 f., they seem to contain an allusion to the death of Dumuzi; at least the phraseology of these lines belongs to the Dumuzi literature; cf. *VS* 2:2 iii 16–18 + *RA*, *8* (1911), 168, ll. 100–02 in a difficult context: ᵍⁱˢhaš hur-e-gu-la edin-é-mùš-a-ka / ki-bi-a guruš ᵍⁱˢmá-gul-gul-a kur-ra ì-dé (=du, *alāku*, weak) / dam-ga-ša-an-an(a)-ka ᵍⁱˢmá-gul-gul-a kur-ra ì-dé.

mah: *ṣīru* "lofty, exalted." an-gim R-a, 123; in-ga-R, 79; aša-R-me-en, 137; te-en-te-bi R-a ("it is sublime . . ."), 39; du₁₁-ga-ni R-a ("that her speaking to . . . was sublime . . ."), 151; cf. 64; šà-kù-zu R-a, 110.

^{gi}ma-sá-ab: *masabbu* "basket," 68. Cf. commentary ad loc.

ma-ra-az: "exuberant, joyous." 146, var. of ma-az, q.v.

ma-az: *hitbuṣu, ulṣu.* See hi-li-R, 146; var.: ma-ra-az.

me: R-gal-gal, 6; R-huš, 23, "terrible me's; negative attributes":
me-te. R-huš-bi "the terrible me's which are fitting," i.e., a merited
punishment; cf. *SGL*, 2:121 f.; R-du$_{10}$-ga, var. of R-šár-ra, 1;
R-imin-bi, 5: "totality of me's"; me-zi, 60. me-zu ... du$_{11}$(*zamāru*),
65; R ba, 152, "bestow the me's," cf. Sjöberg, *Nanna*, p. 117, l. 12;
R gaba ... tab, 8; R hal-hal, cf. Chapter 5, n. 4; R íl, 7; R sì-ma, 14;
R šu-šè ... lá, 7; R-a túm-ma (*šulukat*), 64; R ur$_4$ (*hamāmu*), 8.

me-lám: *mela/emmû* "radiance." R gùr-ru, 2.

me-te: *simtu* "suitability"; R me-huš-bi, with var. me-ta(?), 23, "a
merited punishment."

mè: see igi-R-*ak, 26.

mí: *awīltum*; *sinništum* "woman." A reading mí for SAL is firmly established
(cf. Römer, *SKIZ*, 80) and equally a reading mu-nu-uš, cf. supra s.v.
ku$_4$ and VAT 8381 (unpubl.) 18: [nam-šu]b-eridu^{ki}-ga murgu$^{mu-ur-gu}$
sa-sa-al ti-ti munuš$^{mu-nu-uš}$-bé ù-me-ni-dib; both texts are written
in eme-egi. Note that the instances of mí are all found in compound
words and verbs, in enclitic or proclitic position; munuš is found in
absolute inflection. The two different forms seem to correspond to an
absolute inflection and a compound inflection analogous to the strong and
weak forms of the verbs: 55, 77, 79; R-zi, 2, 65.

mir: *ezzu* "fierce." R-R-zu ga-àm-du$_{11}$, 135.

munuš: see mí.

muru(m)$_x$: muru$_x$-ma-né hu-mu-un-te, 90, is found in a very difficult context; see also tab-ku$_4$. A variant (collated) has: nì-na-ma-né.
The sign seems to be different in different manuscripts, but it is hardly
possible to be sure about the differences in the cursive script. Read perhaps
SAL + LAGAR or SAL.UD.EDIN, which is ^{mí}u$_4$-ru$_6$ = muru$_5$. For te in this
context, see tab-ku$_4$; it certainly implies "to approach a woman." Our
interpretation starts from the observation that Lugalanne committed a sin
by approaching this woman; cf. the quotation from *Šurpu* s.v. tab-ku$_4$.
The variant nì-na-ma (a common syllabic spelling for nì-nam-ma; cf.
e.g. line 85 with variants) suggests that muru(m)$_x$ goes back to mí-ú-
rum, literally "own woman, woman who is one's property," and that
this was, in one textual tradition, confused with nì-ú-rum, "thing
which is one's property," and then replaced by its approximate
synonym, nì-nam (q.v.).

ná: *ṣalālu* "lie down." gìri-ni-šè ì-R, 78.

nag: *šatû* "drink." ba-ra-R-R, 45.

[nam: 1. *šimtu*; 2. sign of abstract and collective.]

nam...kar: "take away the fate / the manhood," 77. Cf. nam-kúr, *šimtam šupēlu*; Ebeling, *Handerhebung* (=VIO 20:60:14), *tu-uš-te-pi(pil)-li ši-ma-tam-ma i-dam-mi-iq lem-nu*; ibid., 128:17 *ša zik-ri u si-in-niš[-ti tuštepelli šimātišun]*; both incantations to Ištar.

nam-ku₅: "curse," 95. Cf. ref. in Römer, *SKIZ* 100–02; Falkenstein, *ZA, 57* (1965), 117, and CH rev. 26:52: *ši-ma-ti-šu li-ru-ur* (cf. Borger, *Or., N.S.* 34:168 f.).

nam-mu: "what is it to me?" 74, 103. Cf. te-àm = nam-mu = *mi-[in-šu]*, *MSL*, 4:42:156 and the remarks of Falkenstein there; YBC 4620:32: dingir-mu za-ra nir im-ta-gál-en ("I trust in you") lú-šè R ("that man, what is he to me," or: "what can I expect from men?"); *ZA, 52* (1957), 17, l. 21.

nam-en: *ēnūtu* "high priesthood." R-na túm-ma, (*šulukat*), 4, 107.

nam-lú-uₓ-lu: *awīlūtu* "mankind." 21.

nam-mah...du₁₁ "exalt." Cf. comment on stanza ix. Vet. Test. Suppl. 3:173:1: nam-mah dingir-ra-na...hé-im-me; *SGL* 2:117: ᵈnisaba nin-ki-umum-ma nam-mah-a-ni bí-in-du₁₁; *BE* 31:12 rev. 13:22 and passim as refrain to Inanna: ᵈnin-é-gal-la ki-ùr-zu mu-gál nam-mah-zu ga-àm-du₁₁; 4R 29 = *OECT* 6:59 rev. 1:13 f.: (Marduk) mu-zu bí-du₁₁ nam-mah-zu bí-du₁₁ = *šum-ka az-kur nar-bi-ka aq-[bi]*; YBC 4620:50 = 8630:17: (Enki) nam-mah-zu ga-àm-du₁₁; YBC 4605:5 (Ninisina?) ... za-da í-gál nam-mah-zu ga-àm-du₁₁. ᵈnanna: 93, 100, 120, 122, 133, 148.

ní: 1. *ramānu* "self." R-bi-a, 46, 47, 48. 2. *puluhtu* "awe." R-me-lám, 21.

ní-te: *palāhu* "fear, respect." ní ba-ra-ba-da-te, 87.

nì: 1. "something, *quidque, quodcumque*." 2. Individualizing sign. 1.: 16, 26, 139; 2.: nì-gig, *ikkibu*, 43; nì-kù-šà-ga-na, 57.

nì-me-gar: *qūlu kūru* "silence"; "acclaim," "the 'perfect tribute'," 22. Cf. Falkenstein *SGL, 1* (1959), 75 f.; van Dijk, *SGL*, 2:19; Reiner, *AS, 16* (1965), 247–51; for the verb me(-gim)-gar: Falkenstein, *ZA, 57* (1965), 87 ad 57, and note the inexplicable R = *išdihu*, *CAD,I*, 234 f.

nì-nam: *mimma šumšu*; "whatever, everything, *quidvis*." R-ma-ni in-kúr, 85.

nì-ur₅-ša₆-ša₆: "sweetness"; "(sexual) happiness," 73. Cf. *Sagesse*, p. 54; Römer, *SKIZ* 31:27; ibid., 197 and frequently in Inanna-Dumuzi texts.

nin: *bēltu* "lady, queen"; voc. nin-mu, 6, 20, 34, 134; nin-bàn-da, 114, paralleling nin-gal, 112. Comparison with nin₉-gal/banda, which occurs in similar contexts, e.g. *JCS, 16* (1962), 80, ll. 6 f., does not suit the context. The only possible interpretation seems to be: Inanna has been from birth on the junior queen, i.e. she has been the nu-gig of the god of Heaven; but now she has been exalted to be the queen of Heaven, taking the place of Antum, sitting with An on the throne of Heaven. This exaltation of Inanna is fully described in in-nin-šà-gur$_4$-ra, *Belleten*, *16* (1952) Pl. LXIII 3:12–20; cf. *Acta Or.* 28:15, n. 28; R gú-tuku, 143; R kur-ra diri-ga, 42; R an-ra diri-ga, 59; R-gal, 112; R-gal-nin-e-ne, *bēlit bēlēti*, 60; R hi-li gú-è, 153; R-kal-kal, 109; R-ki-ága-an-na, 121, 135; R-kur-kur-ra, 62; R-me-šár-ra/du$_{10}$-ga, 1; R šà ì-húl, 40; R un-gal, 138; R ur-ra u$_5$-a, 14; R ur$_5$ i-ša$_6$, 40.

^{d}nin-gal: 149.

nin-me-šàr-ra as epithet of Inanna, 1. ^{d}inanna R-me-en dingir nu-mu-e-da-di: *BE* 31:12 rev. 12, 21, et passim as refrain in this Inanna hymn; cf. *SEM*, 86 f., 89, *STVC* 87. Cf. Kramer, *Enmerkar*, p. 223: in-nin-me-šár-ra kù-^{d}inanna-ke$_4$. Cf. *YOS*, 1:31 (="Warad-Sin 8"): 1–3: ^{d}inanna nin ní-gal-gùr-ru me-šár-ra tab-ba. Cf. also *LKA* 77 ii 2 f. = Ebeling, *ArOr* 21:364:(Ṣarpanitum) nin-gal abzu-a / me-šár-ra šu-du$_7$-a = *šar-<ra>-tú* GAL- *tú šá ap-si-i* / *šá kiš-šat par-ṣe šuk-lu-lat.*

nir-gál: *takālu/tukultu* "rely, reliance." Cf. *SGL* 2:43; R-gú-en-na-ke$_4$, 143.

nita$_x$-dam: *aššatu/mūtu* "spouse," 111.

nu-gig: *harimtu* "hierodule," 151.

nu-gig-an-na: "hierodule of An," 3; this is the "civil state" of Inanna in the Sumerian Pantheon, at least at Uruk; less certainly at Umma, where Šara is her son, and for the Inanna whose son is ^{d}lú-làl; cf. *CT* 42:3 v 53– vi 33, where Inanna seems to be identified with Antum. Cf. s.v. nin, nin-gal; the title may have been applied originally to Inanna; cf. R-ka (ke$_4$) nam-gal-la-(a-)na in-nin-ra šìr-re-(e-)ès ga-(an-) na-ab-bé-en, Römer, *SKIZ* 129:15 f. and other references, ibid., 152 and *CAD,H*, s.v. *harimtu* and *CAD,I*, s.v. *ištaritu*; *RA*, *33* (1936), 104, ll. 2, 14, 25, 28: mu-gib-an-na-mèn; applied to Nanâ, *SLTN* 71:3; to Ninisina, *SRT* 6:2:32 = 7:7: in-nin nu-(u$_8$-)gig-gal-an-na-ke$_4$, cf. Römer, *SKIZ* 204:59 and cf. also Enki and the World, 402. But this is certainly a syncretism.

nu-kúš-ù: "restlessness," 32; deverbal noun, here used, not in the sense of *nukuššû* (for which see Salonen, *Türen*, pp. 69 f.) or *almattu*, but of the Akkadian participle *la ānihu, lanihu* (for which see *AHw*, pp. 48 f.). Cf. Lambert, *BWL* 242:22: gìri-mu nu-kúš-u = *la a-ni-ha še-pa-a-a* and ibid., 249 ad loc. For the nominal construction, cf. *BRM*, 4:9:38 f.: ù-nu-ku i-bí-né i-ma-al / nu-kúš-ù á-na i-ma-al eme-sal, "sleeplessness is deposited on her eyes, restlessness is placed in her arms"; *SBH* 27 rev. 4 f.: R-bi-mèn = *ba'-la' in-na-hu ana-ku.* See gìri-(a) . . . si.

nundum: *šaptu* "lip." R-R-bi-ta ki-su-ub...aka, 116. Cf. *MSL*, 2:57:321, 3:118:260, and note; eme-sal: šu-um-du-um, *SRT* 31:24;

cf. dingir-meš *i-gi₄-gu i-na* nundum-*šu-nu qaq-qa-ra u*[*naššaqū*], *KAR* 306:29; R-bi-a ki-su-ub a-ra-aka-ne, Kapp, *ZA, 51* (1955), 79, ll. 110 f.

pa: *elâtu,* see an-pa above, s.v. an.

PA.AN: see billuda above.

píl/pi-lá: "make obscure/dirty." u₄ mu-da-píl, 70, in parallelism with uₓ-lu . . . dul. Cf. lú-lul-la-ke₄ uₓ-lu mu-un-dul . . . á-nu-zu-(a)-mu ma-ra-pi-lá-en, Vet. Test. Suppl. 3:173:28 f.; *Sagesse,* p. 122, ll. 5 f. Cf. also *ŠL* 172:159 and *AHw,* s.v. *lu"û*(*m*); for píl = *hamāṭu,* cf. *CAD,H,* s.v.

ra: see gù-R-R, 29; sag-giš-R-R, 126.

rá: see šudₓ-rá, 149.

sá-du₁₁: see šu-R, 5.

[sag: *rēšu*]

sag-gá-gá: (*w*)*âru* "proceed." *SGL* 2:30; sag nu-mu-un-dè-gá-gá, 37.

sag-kal: *ašarēdu* "first, foremost." Both readings, sag-rib and sag-kal, are attested. For -rib, cf. Sjöberg, *AfO, 20* (1963), 174, ad Gordon, *Proverbs,* 1:148. sag-ka-al-ᵈnin-urta is attested in *VS* 10:192:11, dupl. VAT 1284:10 (unpubl.): sag-kal; and VAT 8519 rev. 4:20 reads muš-sag-kal-la. Cf. also the personal name é-sag-kal-l[a] in an unpubl. Ur III text.

sag-kešda: *it'udu* "watch, guard." Falkenstein, *ZA, 47* (1942), 215; *49* (1949), 114, l. 7; 120, l. 32; me-gal-gal-la-R-bi, 6.

sag-ki: *pūtu* "forehead, face." R-huš-a, 37.

sag-rib: see sag-kal.

sahar-(da) . . . gi₄: "turn into dust," "in pulverem reverti," euphemism for "to die," 73. Cf. *CAD,E,* s.v. *eperu,* 186b, *tāru ana epri* and, for the meaning here, Gilg. XI 133: *kullat tenišēti itūra ana ṭiṭṭi* (cf. *Acta Or.* 28:43 f.). Cf. also expressions such as sahar-(ta) . . . sár (Kramer, *JCS, 5* [1950–51], 3, l. 44; cf. *SGL* 2:16 f.); sahar-(ta) . . . dúr-(dúr) (*BASOR, SS,* 1:18:220; cf. *AS, 16* [1965], 137p); sahar-ra . . . nigin (*Enmerkar,* 170); sahar-ra . . . bala (cf. *TMH, NF,* 3:36:56 = *SRT* 4:49; YBC 4620:38: sahar-ra nam-bí-ib-bala-e-en); sahar-ta . . . šub (2 Elegies 19), etc. Cf. *SGL* 2:44.

sar: *kuššudu; ṭarādu* "make hurry, chase out." lú-éše R, 50; lú hé-mi-R-re, 91. Cf. *BA, 10* (1913), 42 (= 105):15–18: é-a hé-ni-íb-sar-re = *ina bīti lit-ru-us-su*; YBC 7351: ibila-tur-ra é-ad-da-na-ka íb-ta-an-sar-re nì-gig-ᵈnin-urta-ke₄.

si: 1. *malû; mullû* "be full, fill." 2. *maṣû* "be enough." 1. 49; see gìri(-a) . . . si, 32; 2. See im-ma-si-im-ma-diri-ga, 138.

si-sá: *šutēšuru* "straighten out, prepare," 136.

sì: see sum, below.

si-ig: *sapānu*; *šuqammumu* "strike down, level, silence." Cf. Jacobsen, *ZA*, *52* (1957), 124, n. 71; Gud. Cyl. A viii 4: dul-dul mu-sig; nì ma-ra-ta-si-ig, 26; cf. Römer, *SKIZ*, 163.

sig_x(KA × LI)-gi_4: var. KA × BALAG; *šagāmu* "echo, roar." For the problems connected with the reading of this complex with the known variants KA × LI, KA × ŠED, and KA × BALAG, cf. Falkenstein, *AnOr* 28:32 and the comments of Gordon, *Proverbs*, 69; for the meaning, Falkenstein, *AnOr* 28:123. We continue to transliterate sig_x, as the objections do not seem conclusive. ki-sig_x-gi_4-za, 10; the construction is not immediately evident: "on the place where you . . ." should be *-gi_4-gi_4-za-ka; cf. ki-di-ku_5-da-ka, *NG* 3:127 f.; therefore, we prefer to analyze: *ki-e sig_x-gi_4-gi_4-za, a locative-terminative where we find in an analogous context the accusative, e.g. 4*R* 28:2:11: ^{d}iškur šúr-ra-na ki ši-in-ga-tuk_4-tuk_4; ^{d}iškur-da sig_x . . . gi_4-gi_4, 30 (*ragāmu*). [Cf. now *UET* 6:203:17: u_4 al-du-du še-eg al-gi_4 with variants.]

si-il: *nuttû* "split." Cf. Jacobsen, *ZA*, *52* (1957), 36 ad 26; uru-bi . . . si-il, 94; ka-kešda . . . si-il, 47. Cf. *JCS*, *5* (1950–51), 3, l. 45: za-gìn-$ša_6$-ga-zu za-zadim-ma-ka (with the stone of . . .) nam-ba-da-an-si-il-le.

sila: *sūqu* "street," 25.

silim-ma . . . du_{11}/e: "say hail," 83, 150. Cf. refs. collected by Römer, *SKIZ* 149 f., 203 f., n. 52; see giš-ká-an-na and Schollmeyer, *Šamaš* 7:3 f.: ^{giš}si-gar-kù-an-na-ke_4 silim-ma hu-mu-ra-ab-bé = *ši-gar ša-me-e el-lu-tum šul-ma liq-bu-ku*.

$sín^{mušen}$: *sinuntu* "swallow," 105. Cf. Thureau-Dangin, *RA*, *33* (1936), 109 ad 24: še-na^{mušen} = *si-nun-ti*.

sizkur: *teslītu* "prayer." R . . . šu-ti, 144.

sù: phon. /sudr/. Cf. var. šà-sur- for šà-sù, 65; la-la . . . sù-sù (*ulluhu*), (*litbušu*), 146; see ki-za . . . R, 43.

su_8: *alāku ša mādūti* "go (pl.)," 36, 48. Or translate "stand" with Krecher, *WO* 4:1–11?

su-din^{mušen}: *suttinnu*, "bat"; R-dal-a, 35. Cf. von Soden, *AfO*, *20* (1963), 124.

^{d}su'en: 41, 58, 74.

suh-kešda: *tiqnu* "ornament." R-gal-gal-la, 3 (possessive use: "who possesses the great ornaments"). Cf. PN en-suh-kešda-an-na, Edzard, *ZA*, *53* (1959), 18, n. 43; Römer, *SKIZ* 158 ad 3; an attribute of Inanna, cf. Langdon, *AfK*, *1* (1923), 26 f. [=1^2:18]36; 38 [=Sidersky, *RA*, *26* (1929), 29, ll. 36, 38; cf. Scheil, *ZA*, *10* (1895), 293, ll. 35–37]: *zi-im-ru-ša du-uš-šú-pu ra-bu-ú ti-iq-nu*.

sum: *nadānu* "give," strong form; weak: sì. The attested spellings are not consistent; note sum^{šu} in *CT* 42:4:17 (cf. Kramer, *JCS*, *18* [1964], 39,

No. 20) and VAT 8381 (unpubl.):4: ^{e}a-šà-ge ri-a ka-kešda$^{ki-ši}$ lú-ra hé-sum^{šu}-mu; but cf. ibid. 14: (asalluhi) igi im-ma-an-sì^{zi}; ha-ba-ab-R-mu, 93; gír ba-da-ra ma-an-R, 108.

^{d}sun-zi: R-mu, 91: either the name of Inanna at Ur, or dingir; sun-zi, attested as epithet of Inanna.

sur: var. of /sudr/ = sù, q.v.

šà: *libbu* "heart, mind." R-íb-ba, 38; R-hul-gál-la, 39; R ì-húl, 40 (possessive use); nì-kù-R-ga-na, 57; R-kù, 61, 110; R-sù, 65 (*rēmēnû*); gub-ba-R-ga-na, 80; R . . . še$_4$, 80, 121, 137; R ki-bé . . .gi$_4$, 145. See zi-R-gál-la, 92.

šà-X-*ak: prepositional use; *šà-tùr-bi-ak-ta, 54.

šà-gan: see guruš-R, 50.

ša$_6$: *damāqu*; ša$_6$-ga: *damiqtu* "favor." ša$_6$-ga . . . du$_{11}$/e, 55; see ur$_5$-R below.

šár: "3600, all." See nin-me-R-ra, 1.

še$_8$: *bakû* "cry," 24. See ír-še$_8$-še$_8$.

še$_4$(d): *šupšuhu* "cool." See šà-R, 80, 121, 137.

še(g): *magāru* "agree, obey." en-na-nu-R-ga, 131.

šèg: *zanānu* "rain." izi . . . R-gá, 13.

šeg$_x$: see GÍR.

[šìr: *zamāru*]

šìr-kù: *širkugû* "sacred song, incantation," 63, 99; cf. comment ad loc. tu$_6$-tu$_6$ nam-šub-šìr-kù-ga u-me-ni-šid = *ta šìr-kù-ga-e mu-nu-ma*, 5R 50:63 f. = Schollmeyer, *Šamaš* 33:66 f.; *SGL* 1:123:57: nar-re R-ga im-mi-in-du$_{11}$; Gud. Cyl. B iv 6: . . .^{d}nanše R inim-zu é-e ba-an-du$_{11}$; cf. Falkenstein, *ZA, 49* (1949), 86, n. 2; "Enki and the World," 104: abzu-gá R-nam-šub ma-an-lá; cf. Falkenstein, *ZA, 56* (1964), 64 f.

šu: *qātu* "hand." šu-zu-šè . . . lá, 7.

šu-ba: weak form of šu-bar, q.v.; 83 (var.).

šu-bar: *wuššuru* "release," 83.

šu-a . . . gi$_4$-gi$_4$: *šunnû* "repeat," 140. *ŠL* 354:149g; *OECT* 6, Pl. XX and p. 4, K. 4812:1 f.: inim-mu šu-a ga-ni-íb-gi$_4$ nì šu nu-gi$_4$-gi$_4$ = *a-ma-ti lu-šà-an-ni ul šà šu-un-ni*; ibid., Pl. IX K. 5271:7 f.: šu-gi$_4$-a-mu-dè = *ina šu-un-ni-ia*; ibid., p. 36:21 f. = 4R 27:3:42–45: inim-mu ga-mu-ra-ab-du$_{11}$ inim-mu hur nu-gi$_4$-gi$_4$-e-dè = *a-ma-ti lu-šá-an-ni a-ma-ti ul šà šu-un-ni-e* (hur + neg. = "never," cf. *SGL* 2:92). Cf. for the ref. Falkenstein, *ZA, 44* (1938), 19; *ŠL* 401:129 presumably refers to this same passage. Cf. also *SGL* 2:148: ^{d}en-ki engur-ra-[ke$_4$] šu-a-aš an-na-an-gi = *a-na* ^{d}*é-a ina ap-si-i šu-un-ni-šum-ma*.

šu-lá: *kasû* "bind (the hands)," 118. Cf. VAT 8379 (unpubl.) 5:9 ff.: am-dab$_5$-ba-gim šu ba-e-lá / šilam-dab$_5$-ba-gim á-né šu ba-e-lá (gír-tab incantation); *AHw*, s.v. *kasû*; šu-lá = *eṣēlu* = šu(-a)-lá "be paralyzed, folded, idle (said of hands)." Cf. also KAR 375 rev. 3:11–12: šu ba-ab-lá = *uš-te-'e-lá: šute"ulu* "wring the hands"; cf. šu-lá šu-bar-re-da . . . za-e-da ì-[gál], 4*R* 17 obv. 36. Cf. also R = *hašāhu*, *CAD,H*, 134d, *AHw*, p. 332, and above, Chapter 5, note 59.

šu-luh: *šuluhhu* "lustration." R . . . si-sá, 136; R-an-kù-ga, 85. Cf. [iz]i-ur₅ šu-luh-mah-zu si ma-ra-an-sá-e, *UET* 6/1:67:31 (Römer, *SKIZ* 109 restores [gi]š-ur₅); Gud. Cyl. A x 8: šu-luh si bí-sá.

šu-sá-du₁₁: "attain." me-imin-bé R-ga, 5.

šu-šè . . . LÁ: *ina qātē šuqallulu*, "attach to, suspend from the hands," 7. Cf. *SEM*, 1 ii 4 = *TRS* 24 rev. 6' = *CT* 15:43:7 f.: am-ti-la šu-bi-šè (i)ⁱ-im-lá = *ri-mu bal-ṭa ina qa-ṭi-šu uš-qa-lal-šu*; for the reading cf. sur₅ = *šuqallulu*: *ŠL* 2:481:44; Gordon, *Proverbs*, 2.66, n. 7.

šu-ti: [ti weak form of te(g)]: *leqû*; šu ba-e-re-ti, 23; sizkur(-a) . . . R, 144.

šud$_x$(KA × ŠU)-rá: *karābu*, 149.

šu-ùh-a . . . DU: *ešû* "confuse, disconcert." (Cf. *CAD,E*, s.v.) Var. šu-šùh-a . . . DU₁₁, 72; DU here probably the "weak" form; cf. *SGL* 2:81:10 and ibid., 92 f.: šu-šùh-a . . . di and šu-šùh-a . . . du₁₁.

tab: see gaba-R, 8.

tab-ku₄: (var. dab₅-ku₄), 90; this compound(?) verb is found in a difficult context; it is reminiscent of the catalogue of sins in *Surpu* II (see above, Chapter 5, note 49). Here, however, the subject is said to be "entering before you" (*mu-e-ši-n-kur-a-ani, pronominal conjugation); tab therefore cannot be the indirect object (*ana tappê*). It cannot be the direct object either, since we would then expect a comitative infix. The sense required is "as a partner" or in "unison," and we have a kind of adverbial compound: "entered together." Cf. several parallel constructions in the difficult passage *VS* 10:123 ii 7 ff.; here šu tab-dù . . . me-ri tab-sì must mean "joined hands (with her), put his feet/legs together (with her)," and tab-húl thus means "rejoiced together," tab hi-li-dù, "made attractive together."

tag₄: *ezēbu* "leave"; "divorce." uru mu-ta-ab-R-e, 79; má . . . ki-kúr-ra hé-bí-in-R, 98.

tar: see èn-tar.

te(y): "approach." Weak form: ti; see šu-ti above; muru$_x$-ma-né . . . R, 90. See *sub* tab-ku₄; u₄-dè . . . R, 70, 71 (in 70 gizzu is also subject: parallelismus membrorum with omission of the subject in the first verse).

[te-en: *balû* (*CAD,B*, s.v.); is this the same root as *ten "slant" (for which see Christian, MVAG 18:56–58)? See me-te above.]

te-en-te(-en): *balû, bullû* "assuage, extinguish"; šà . . . R, 142; šà-íb-ba . . . R, 38; šà-hul-gala₇ . . . R, 39; íb-ba . . . R, 41.

ti: weak form of te(g), q.v.

ti(1): *balāṭu* "live," 69.

til: *gamāru* "finish, cease." hi-li . . . ba-ra-mu-un-R, 88; see di-R, 117.

tu-ud: *alādu* "give birth to (a song)," 138. Cf. commentary ad loc. and the Socratic or maieutic (i.e. midwifery) method. See u_4-tu-ud-da below.

tug_4: var. of tag_4, 79, 98.

tuku: see gú-R.

túm: 1. *šuluku* "fit." me-a R-ma, 64; cf. Sjöberg, *Nanna-Suen*, p. 108, l. 1 and 110 ad loc.; nam-en-na-R-ma, 4; for en-me-a-R-ma Unug^{ki}-ga as epithet of Bur-Sin, cf. *BE* I 19, *AOS* 43:8. 2. *(w)abālu*, *tabālu* "carry (off)." See ki-za-R, 42, 59; me-R-ma, 64 var. Cf. *Enmer-kar*, 57 f.: gá-e abzu-ta zà-mí du_{11}-ga-mu-dé / eridu^{ki}-ta me R-a-mu-dè and the references collected by Römer, *SKIZ* 153 ad loc.; *STVC* 36:9: nin-mu an-šà-ta me mu-e-túm (cf. Sjöberg, *Nanna*, p. 37); *CT* 42:12 (Kramer, *PAPhS*, *107* [1963], 503 ff.) and 22. 3. See šu-ùh-a . . . DU above.

tùr: *tarbaṣu* "byre, sacred byre," 54. tùr in this context can hardly be equated with an ordinary "cow stall" or even with that of the temple cattle. This tùr seems to play a role in religious and social life: perhaps marriage was consummated there, perhaps a part of sexual life was restricted to these houses, as it is known from other primitive cultures; cf. above, Chapter 5, note 22.

u_4: 1. "day; daylight." 2. "storm." 1. R-dalla-è, var. u_4-bar, 1; R . . . du_{10}, 146; R mu-da-píl, 70; R-dè . . . te, 70; 71, see te; 2. u_4-dè á . . . sì, 17; R gù . . . ra-ra, 29; R . . . du_7-du_7, 28.

u_4-bar: var. of u_4, 1; cf. Sjöberg, *Nanna-Suen*, p. 128.

u_4-tu-ud-da: "birthday." *SLTN* 78 rev. 2:22: u_4-tu-da-mu u_4-hé-gál-la-[ka]m; *UET* 8:70:11 = YBC 4705:13: u_4-tu-da-mu-ta ^{d}utu-ra ù-na-a-du_{11}, var. ù-ne-[dè-dah].

u_5: *rakābu* "ride, mount." ur-ra R-a, 14.

u_x(GIŠGAL): see lú-u_x-lu; ùlu.

u_6: *naplusu* "glance." R-zi-dè-eš . . . è, 148.

ug_4: *mātu* "die." ì-R-ge-dè-eš, 99.

ugnim: *ummānu* "army," 46.

ugu(n): *alādu* "give birth." See a-a-R, 52; ama-R, 61.

ukù: *nīšu* "people," 45.

ukù-lu-a: *nīši dišātu* "multitudes." zi-gál-R, 63. Cf. *SGL* 2:61; Römer, *SKIZ* 14:41; 91:31; 131:181; *CAD,D*, 129c: di-ku_5 R = *daiān ni-ši da-ša-a-i*[*te*]; ka-R-bi = *ina pi nīši di-šá-a-ti*.

ulù/u_x-lu: *alû* "sandstorm." ní-me-lám u_x-lu-da, 21; the postposition is ambiguous. 1. For -da with "Verben der Gemütsbewegung" cf. Falkenstein, *GSGL* 2:143 f. and note é-babbar-da ní-te-gá (var. ní-tug) passim in inscriptions of Warad-Sin and Rim-Sin; this would

imply that nì-me-gar-huš-bi of ll. 22 is such a *verbum sentiendi*, albeit
in the form of a kind of pronominal conjugation: "(in) their fear of . . ."
2. For -da as copula ("and"), cf. Poebel, *GSG*, §§ 399 f.; note that this use
is frequent in inscriptions of Sargonic date (e.g. *BE* 1/2), but rare in
later texts.

ulù/u$_x$-lu-da . . . dul "cover with a storm," 71. Cf. *SGL* 2:75:11
nu-še-ga u$_x$-lu dul-ù. Vet. Test. Suppl. 3:173:28: lú-lul-la-ke$_4$
u$_x$-lu mu-un-dul and the refs. *CAD,A,/*1:375 f.

ù-ma: *irnittu*; R-gub-gub "attain victory, triumph," 104, 132. Cf. ref.
in Sjöberg, *ZA*, *54* (1961), 66, n. 43; as epithet of Inanna: *SBH* 56 rev.
65 f. = YBC 9862 rev. 6: 5-(u)-kam-ma mu ù-ma gub-gub = *ha-an-šu*
<*šumi*> *ir-ni-t*[*i* . . .], referring to Inanna's names; YBC 4665 rev. 17 f.:
in-nin-e ki ù-ma gub-bu-ba-šè sá-du$_{11}$-ga-àm / ^{d}inanna-ke$_4$
ditto.

ù-na: see gi$_6$-ù-na.

un-gal: *šarratu*; *šurbû*; nin un-gal, 138, probably means *bēltu šurbûtu*,
for which cf. *ŠL* 312:17 and Mullo Weir, *Lex.*, pp. 352 f.; un-gal-
nibru^{ki} as an epithet of Inanna, cf. Goetze, *JCS*, *17* (1963), 129, l. 1;
Falkenstein, *BiOr*, *9* (1952), 88; *SGL* 1:113 f.; cf. *RA*, *12* (1915), 82, 43 f.:
un-gal-nibru^{ki} mu-sa$_4$-a-zu hé-em = ^{d}*šar-rat ni-ip-pú-ru ana šu-*
me-ki lu na-ba-a-tú; *ZA*, *39* (1930), 259, l. 15:9 R-an-ki-a (=I. of
Uruk); *UET* 1:171:1 (=Ningal); *OECT* 6:5:7: R ^{d}pa$_4$-nun-na-an-ki;
SBH 12 rev. 19: hi-li R ^{d}e$_4$-ru$_6$-e . . .; *LKA* 77 ii 5 f.: R$^!$-an-ki-a
R-^{d}a-nun-na-ke$_4$-e-ne = UN.GAL AN-*e u* KI-*tim šar-rat* ^{d}*a-nun-na-ki*,
cf. Falkenstein, *AS*, *16* (1965), 138(t); Landsberger, *MSL*, 2:65 ad 419:
un-gal < nun-gal = nin-gal.

ur: *kalbu* "a beast." ur-gim adda$_x$-kú, 127; R-ra u$_5$-a, 14, "mounted
on a beast"; cf. *Belleten*, *16* (1952), Pl. LXIII iii 12: ur-gal-gal imin-bi
ba-e-u$_5$ an-na ba-è-dè; ibid., i 22 ^{d}inanna pirig-gi-il-gi-il-la
("intertwined" or gal-gal?) dúr-re.

úr: *išdu*; see an-úr.

ur$_4$: *hamāmu* "gather." me . . . R, 8.

ur$_5$: *mešrētu*; *kabattu*; *libbu* "limbs, liver, heart, (seat of the) emotions."
< mur, cf. murgu < mur-gú and murub < mur-ub; nin ur$_5$ i-ša$_6$,
40.

ur$_5$-ša$_6$: *mešrētu damqā*, cf. *SBH* 12 rev. 24; *Sagesse*, p. 54; nin ur$_5$ ì-ša$_6$
(=possessive use "lady, sweetheart"), 40; for the parallelism with šà, cf.
Römer, *SKIZ* 21:10: 14 = YBC 4609 (*BiOr*, *23* [1966], 244) 10, 16:
^{d}i. ur$_5$-re hu-mu-e-húl-le (var. ga-mu-u$_8$-húl-le) ^{d}i. šà-zu hé-
mu-e-húl-le (var. hé-em-); Civil, *Studies Presented to Oppenheim*,
p. 70, l. 63 ur$_5$-me bí-ša$_6$ šà-me bí-húl; ibid., p. 71, ll. 75 f.

uraš: see an-R.

uru: *ālu* "city," 49, 51, 79. Var. urú, 49, 79, 94.

usan: an-usan: *šimetan, da'ummatu,* "evening." Cf. Römer, *SKIZ* 151 (11), 14, var. of an.

ù-sun: *rīmtu,* "wild cow." Cf. *Or., N.S.* 23:233; R-zi-zi-i, 58.

úš: *damu,* "blood"; R ... túm/tùm, var. dé, 45. Cf. ref. in *CAD,D,* s.v. *damu* for *dama umtalli* (=si-si); dé is here not dé = *šapāku,* but the weak form of túm; cf. s. túm. úš ... túm like a ... túm, is an idiomatic use (cf. *bibil libbi*) and means "the water increased," resp. "blood rose in"; the line is probably an allusion to Sukkaletuda, cf. Kramer, *ArOr* 17/1:404: 3:27 f.: pú-kalam-ma-ka úš bi-ib-si-si / pú-kiri$_x$(SAR)-kalam-ma-ka úš-àm ì-túm-tùm, "she filled the wells of the nation with blood, in the wells it was blood that rose."

uš$_x$(KA × ÚŠ) ... sì, var. uš$_x$(KA × ŠU): "throw venom on ...," 9. Cf. *SGL* 2:20; Römer, *SKIZ* 89; uš$_x$ sì-mu = *i[m-tu na-di-tum], CAD,I,* 139b; cf. ibid., 139 f. for its relation to ušumgal; for uš$_7$, written KA × LI, cf. *MSL,* 2:57:325 and *TLB* 2:3:7 = *SGL* 2:31 = Sjöberg, *ZA, 54* (1961), 57, l. 7: lú-nu-še-ga ⸢uš$_7$⸣-nam-úš-a ba-ab-sì-me-en.

ušumgal: *ušumgallu* "dragon," 9.

^{d}ušumgal-an-na, 111.

za$_x$: see hé-zu-hé-za$_x$.

za-a-kam ... du$_{11}$: *kûmma qabû/zamāru/šasû* "say: it-is-thine." R bí-in-du$_{11}$-ga, 122, 133. Type of composition or refrain in honor of various deities; see hé-zu-hé-za$_x$. (1) To Inanna: in Enheduanna B, a succession of at least twenty-eight lines ends ^{d}inanna za-(a)-kam = *ku-(um-)ma eštar.* Cf. *SGL* 2:90, n. 27 and *ZA, 52* (1957), 312 and n. 2. (2) Utu: a chorus of ten lines each ending za-a-kam followed by at least nine lines beginning ^{d}utu za-da-nu-me-a, var. za-da-nu-è, *TRS* 79:29 ff. = *PBS* 1/2:118 rev. ii 5 ff. A similar passage is found in hymns to (3) Nisaba, *OECT* 1:36 i (=*SAHG* 6) 22–31 and (4) Enlil, *SGL, 1* (1959), 16 f.: 108–28. The creative power of Enlil is well known from the e-ne-ém-litanies and from a nine-line ki-ru-gú bracketed by the refrain (?) za-e bí-du$_{11}$ (za-e bí-du$_{11}$), *CT* 42:26:9–19, which is missing in the bilingual duplicates *SBH* 58 obv. 5–22 and *BA* 5:617 = ibid., 544 f. (5) Nanna: at least seven lines ending in ^{d}nanna-kam, Sjöberg, *Nanna-Suen,* pp. 45 f. (6) Marduk: chorus of five lines ending za-a-ke$_4$ = *ku-um-mu,* and followed, after an interval of four lines, by five others beginning with za(-e)-ra or za-e, Langdon, *OECT* 6: 58 f. = 4R 29:1; cf. also the standard Marduk doxology: ša$_6$-ga zíl-zíl-le-bi za-a-kam = *bunnû dummuqu kûmma CAD,B,* 91a; D 61c and Meek, *BA, 10* (1913), 13, ll. 5–12; Delitzsch, ibid., 133. za-a-kam corresponds to za-e-me-en in the hymns of praise, as gá-a-kam corresponds to gá-e-me-en in self-predications, e.g. in the enumeration of Inanna's sanctuaries, *PBS* 5:157

(+dupl.) and cf. the refrain in *-āku* in Gössmann, *Era-Epos* 1:109–14. za-a-kam became a noun, like hé-zu-hé-za$_x$ and is preserved in the omens of Sargon, cf. above, Chapter 1, and n. 24. For refs. and various forms, cf. Römer, *SKIZ* 248; *AHw*, pp. 496 f. s.v. *kú(m)*; *MSL*, 4:62:12.

zalzal-ga: reading of UD.UD-*ga* = *nuwwuru*. Cf. Edzard, *ZA*, *55* (1963), 266, *CAD,B*, 93d (*dummuqu*); *SGL* 2:90, n. 27; mí-zi-R-ga, *nāwirtu*, 65; en-R-ga, 120.

zà-mí: "praise," 153.

za-pa-ág (<zi-pa-ág = *napištu*): *rigmu* "noise, sound," 20.

zé-er: *neheḷṣû*, see gìri-zé-er.

[zi: *napištu*].

zi-gala$_7$: *šiknāt napišti*; R-ùku-lu-a, 63. zi-gala$_7$ has two meanings: 1. "having life," "living being," cf. Römer, *SKIZ* 172 ad 98; but a translation "in/for the living beings (and) the prosperous people" does not yield sense in our context. 2. Cf. *CAD,G*, 21c: zi-ma-al = *ga-mil na-piš-ti*, "granting life," and ibid. 22d; cf. already Thureau-Dangin, *SAKI* 214(b), who cited this equation ad "Warad-Sin 7":3. Cf. also the epithet of Ezinu: zi-sag-gi$_6$-ga in "Enki and the World," 330. R-ukù-lu-a is used, as vocative epithet, in a similar sense. See also next entry.

zi-šà-gala$_7$: *zišagallû* "sustenance," 92. Cf. *CAD,Z*, s.v.; R has the same differentiation of meanings as zi-gala$_7$: "having life in the body" and "granting life to," not so much as "encouragement" (cf. ibid.), but as "food"; cf. *TLB* 2:2:52: har-ra-an-na zi-šà-gala$_7$-zu gá-me-èn and esp. Cattle and Grain 35 (*SRT* 24 + *HAV* 6 + *BE* 31:15) nam-lú-u$_x$-lu zi šà im-ši-íb-gál "they gave sustenance to mankind." Gud. Cyl. A iii 13: zi šà mu-ši-ni-gál. Cf. also YBC 7196:7 = Römer, *SKIZ* 33:69 (*BiOr*, *23* [1966], 245 f.): R uru^{ki}-ni-šè al-di-me-en. For ki-R as epithet of Uruk, cf. above, Chapter 5, note 52.

zi-kú: "consume life." zi-mu um-mi-kú, 105; this idiom must be different from *CT* 17:19:i:25 f.: zi-ni-ta (tés) in-da-an-kú-kú ki-nam-úš ba-an-kešda = *it-ti na-pi-iš-ti-šú i-tak-kal it-ti mu-u-ti ra-kis* "with his throat he swallowed continuously, he was bound up with death"; the verb has a meaning similar to zi . . . ir and zi . . . DU; cf. for the former, *AHw*, s.v. *ašāšu* III; Römer, *SKIZ* 113; above, s.v. im-ma-si-im-ma-diri-ga. Kramer, *Vet. Test. Suppl.* 3:175:72: zi-mu mi-ni-DU-DU(=ir$_{10}$-ir$_{10}$); Gadd, Driver AV 62:13: zi-ni . . . DU; *ZA*, *50* 1952), 66, l. 35 (?); Lugalbanda + Anzu, 126: šà-du$_{11}$-ga-ta zi-mu ma-ra-DU (?). Cf. also *BWL* 245:47: zi-mu ma-da-lúgud-da = *ik-te-ru na-pi*[*š-ti*].

zi(d): *kēnu* "true, right(eous), appropriate." aga-R, 4, 107; dingir-R, 64; me-R, 60; mí-R, 2, 65.

zi-zi: doubled weak form of zig = *tebû*; ù-sun-R-i, 58. Cf. *SGL* 2:75:9;
   HAV 4 obv. 7: mu-na-zi-zi-i-zi; *BE* 29/1, p. 71, n. 2: [^{d}en]-líl-le
   gù ba-an-dé sag-bi zi-zi-dam; i-zi zi-zi-dam i-zi (izi) gá-gá
   (=gin-gin, weak form = *alāku*)-dam, cf. *SGL* 2:55. The verbal form
   zi-zi-i may be explained as the weak form of zig (doubled = *marû*) +
   ed: *zi-zi-ed.
zu: *edû* "know," 16. See gal-zu and hé-zu-hé-za$_x$, above.

Addenda

1. The crucial line 90: tab mu-ši-in-ku$_4$-ra-ni muru$_x$-ma-né hu-mu-un-te requires some additional comments. It is clear that the subject of the pronomial construction, "having entered together with ... before you (Inanna)," must be the same as that of the preceding verbs, i.e. Lugalanne. It is equally evident that Lugalanne, by approaching his muru$_x$ (SAL. LAGAR) committed a sin for which he is roundly cursed by Enheduanna. Since muru$_x$ is a kinship term, Lugalanne's offence must have involved an illicit sexual advance. No other sense of te(ĝ) fits the context. Now Lugalanne, as en of Uruk, was dam-^{d}inanna, "bridegroom of Inanna;" Enheduanna, as en of Ur, was dam-^{d}nanna, "bride of Nanna." Since Inanna of Uruk is indubitably the daughter of Nanna, this yields the following cultic relationship:

$$\text{Enheduanna (en-}^d\text{nanna)} = {}^d\text{Ningal} \sim {}^d\text{Nanna}$$
$$\qquad\qquad\qquad\qquad\quad |$$
$$\qquad\qquad\qquad {}^d\text{Inanna} \sim \text{An} = \text{Lugalanne (en-unug}^{ki})$$

once it is conceded that, in the Sargonic theology, Inanna-Ištar did in fact become the wife of An, replacing Ki (mother earth), or becoming identified with her. This very exaltation is clearly alluded to in our composition, ll. 112–114: by birth, Inanna had been nin-bàn-da, "the junior queen;" now she has become nin-gal, "the senior queen." It is also the main theme of Enheduanna's other great hymn to Inanna, in-nin-šà-gur$_4$-ra (see glossary s.v. nin). In cultic terms, Uruk became ki-nin, "the queen-place," Sargon pa$_4$-šeš-an-na, the "male in-law of An," and Enheduanna muru$_x$, the "female in-law" of An and, by extension, of Lugalanne, the en of Uruk who represented An in the sacred marriage at Uruk.

Thus Lugalanne's sin consisted in his sexual designs, not on Inanna or the priestess playing her role, but on Enheduanna.

2. The analogy to Mansium (above p. 56 and n. 41) may be more complicated than at first appeared. The spelling *man-an-si-um* actually occurs in only one published version of the Curse of Agade (TRS 66:33; so also YBC 4611, unpubl.); it has been compared to the royal name *man-sum* in a historical omen (*KAR* 344 obv.[¹]1) by Güterbock, followed by Falkenstein, *ZA*, *57* (1965), 89.

An unpublished duplicate (YBC 7171) has instead what appears to be *ma-⌜an-ù-um⌝* or *ma-⌜an-nin-um⌝*, suggesting comparison with *ma-ni-u[m]* or *ma-ni-d[an]*, the en of Magan mentioned in an inscription of Naram-Sin from Susa and generally equated with *ma-nu-um* or *ma-an-nu-da-an-nu*, king of Magan in the historical traditions about Naram-Sin (Hallo, *Titles* 6, 67; Hirsch, AfO 20:17 n. 182; 24 f.)

The spelling *ma-an-si-um* recurs in line 68 of "Inanna and Ebih" (cf. UET 6:14:19) with the variants *ma-si-um*, *ma-si-ú*, and ⁿᵍⁱˢma-an-si-um (ref. courtesy B. Eichler). The last of these variants suggests a kind of wood or a wooden implement or article of furniture rather than a personal name in this context, which mentions a throne (ᵍⁱˢgu-za suhuš-gi-na) in the next line. While such a meaning hardly fits the passage in "The Curse of Agade," it nonetheless seems possible that some (late) scribes so understood or misunderstood the word here because here too it is followed by "the throne of kingship" (ᵍⁱˢgu-za-nam-lugala).

Thus the analogy with Lugalanne survives, but in the history of both compositions there was a tendency to lose sight of the fact that personal names were involved.

General Index

SUMERIAN TERMS

ambar, 55
dab₅-ku₄, 57
dingir, 50, 66
dingir-sag-du, 66
du₈, 57
edin, 55
é-mùš, 64
en, 54
ga-, 54
gal, 61
-gim, 51
ha-, 54
(i)n-ga-, 56
ki-ša₆-ga, 55
ki-sì-ga, 55
lugal, 66
lú-sa-gaz, 65

mah, 61
me, 4, 48 f., 53, 63
nam-ᵈen-líl, 65
nam-tag, 57
nin, 53
nu-(u₈)-gig-an-na, 50
pa₄-šeš-an-(na), 7
sahar, 55
šu . . . gi₄-gi₄, 62
šu-ùh-a, 55
tab-ku₄, 57
tùr, 53
umun-é-mùš, 65
ur₅-šà, 52
za-(a-) kam, 3
zà-mí, 3, 63

AKKADIAN TERMS

gipāru, 8, 54
habbātu, 65
illilūtu, 51, 65

šaggāšu, 65
šā'ilu, 55
šutahhû (šuta''û), 57

Plates

Plate 1 CBS 7847 + UM 29.15.422
Obverse and Right Edge

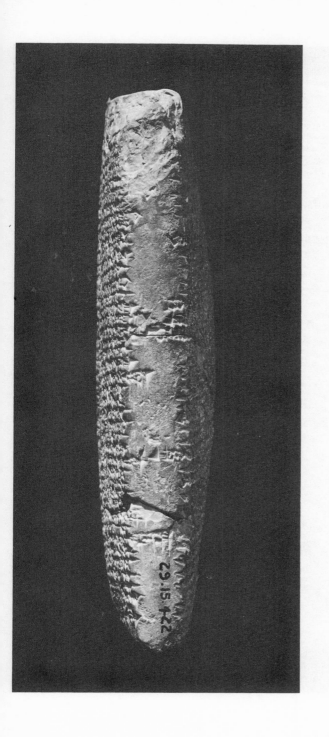

Plate 2   CBS 7847 + UM 29.15.422
Reverse and Right Edge

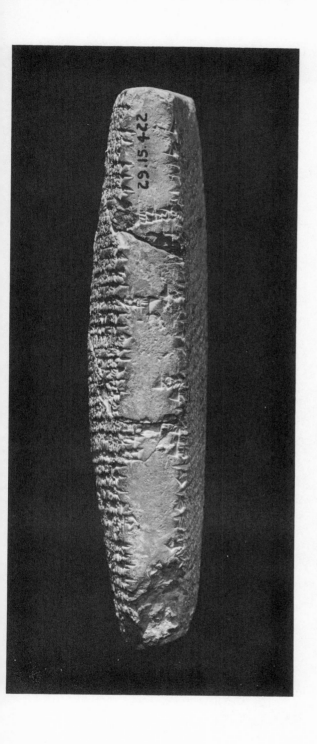

Plate 3   CBS 7847 + UM 29.15.422
Upper Edge

IM 44336

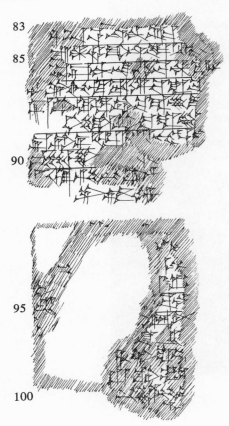

Plate 4 YBC 4656
Obverse

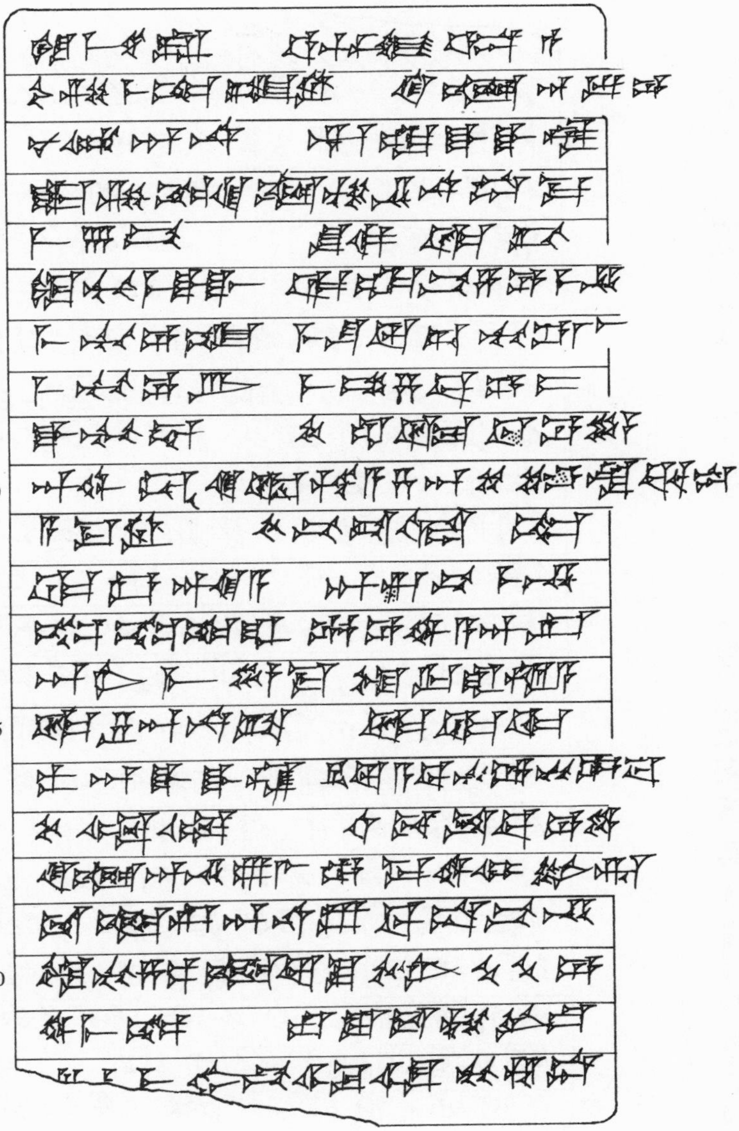

Plate 5 YBC 4656
Reverse

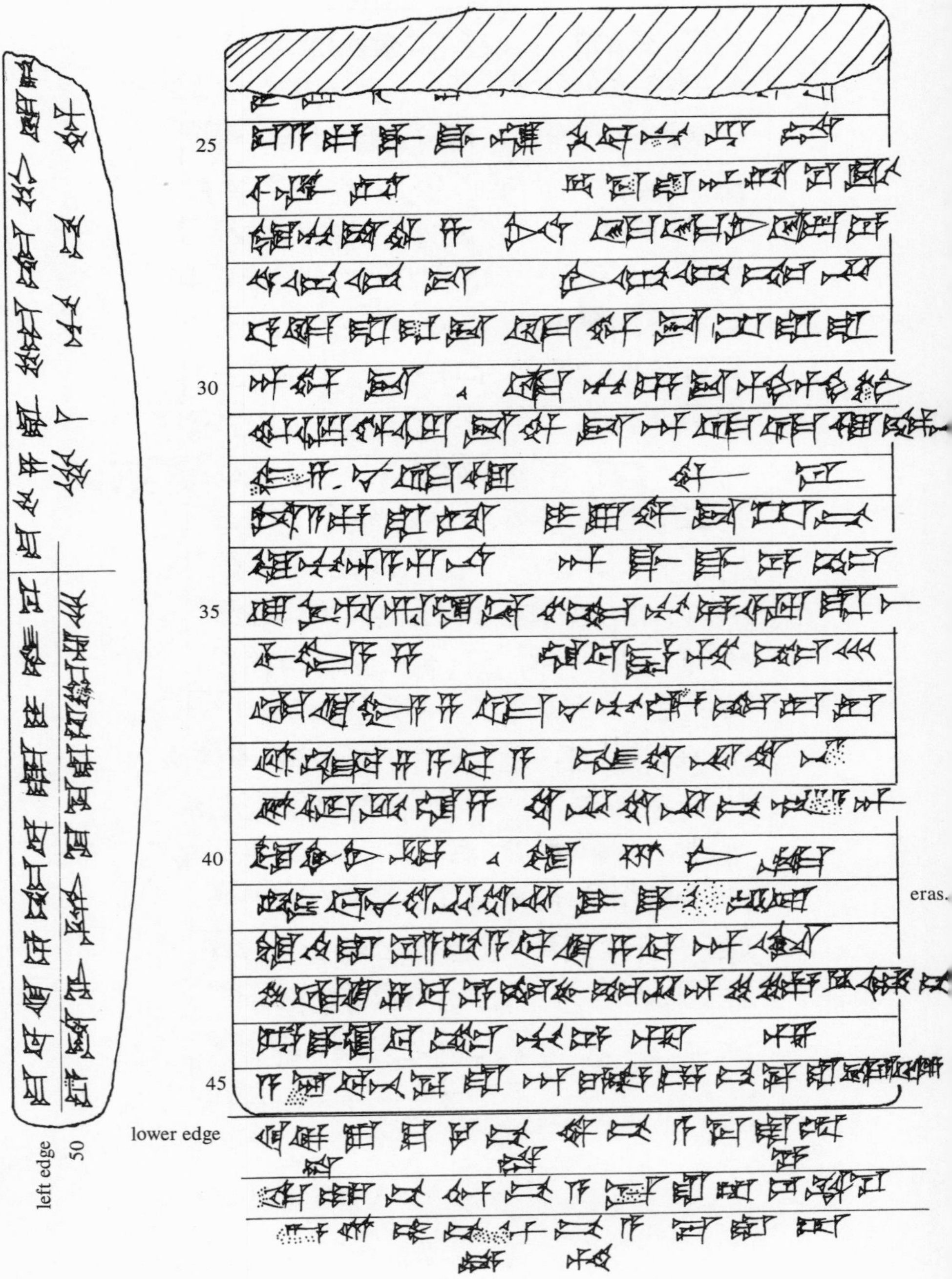

25

30

35

40

eras.

45

left edge

50

lower edge

Plate 6   YBC 7169
Obverse

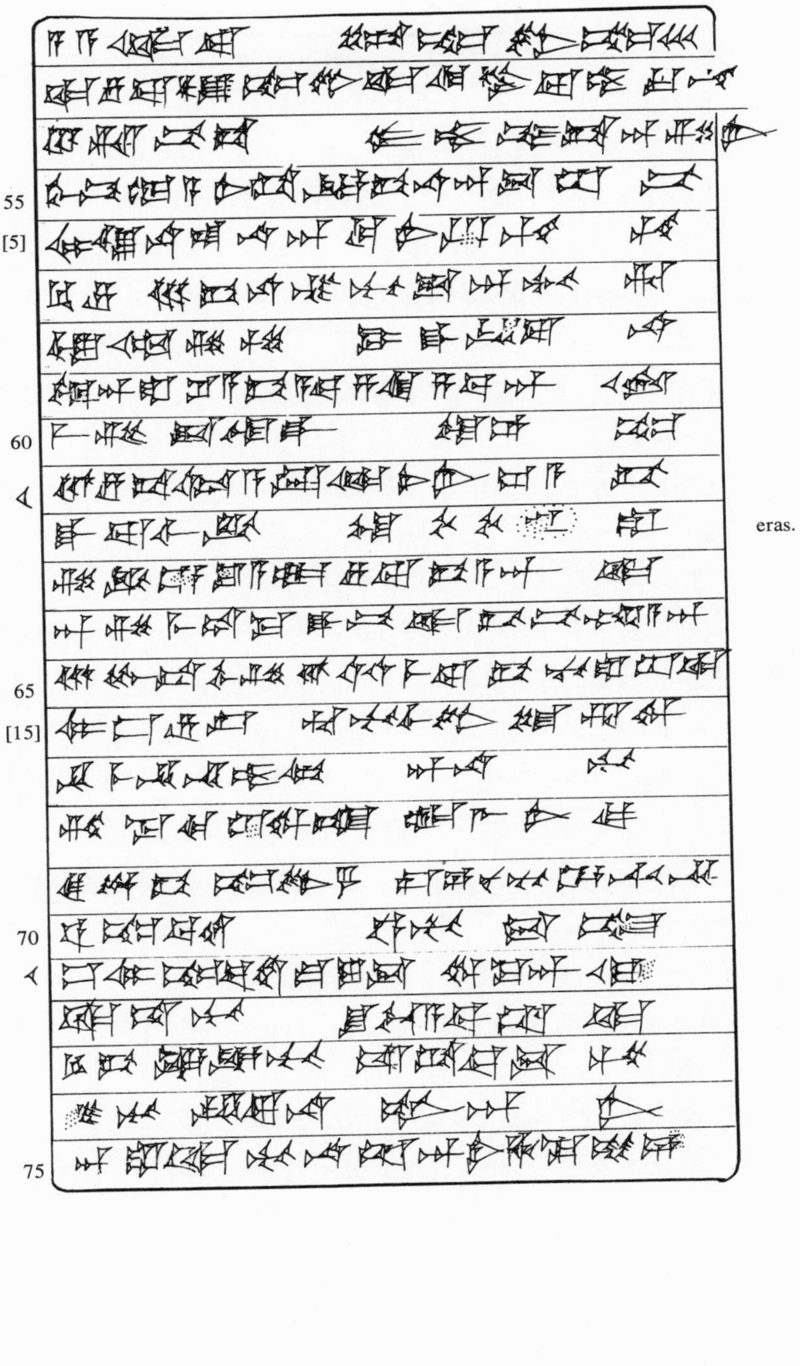

Plate 7 YBC 7169
Reverse

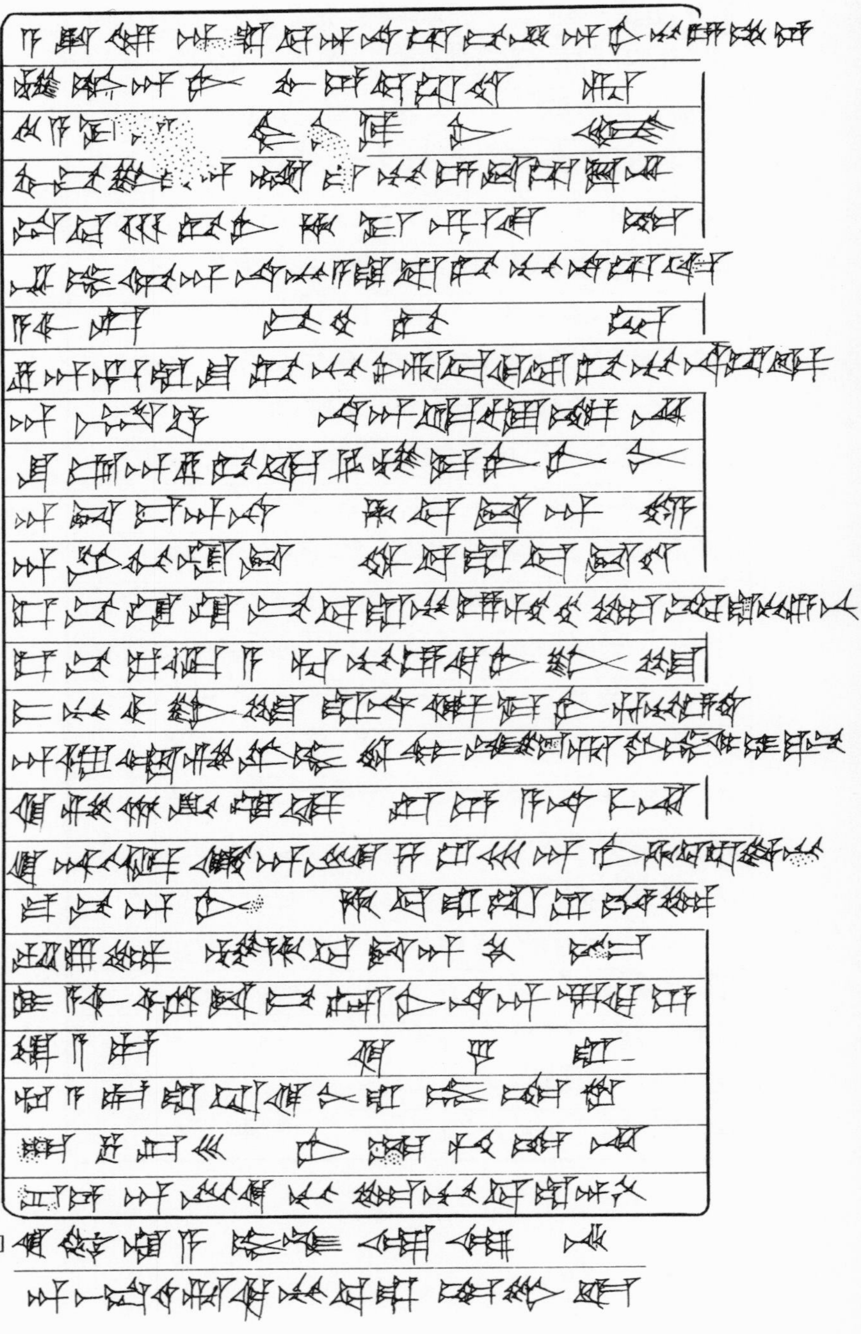

lower edge

Plate 8 YBC 7167
Obverse

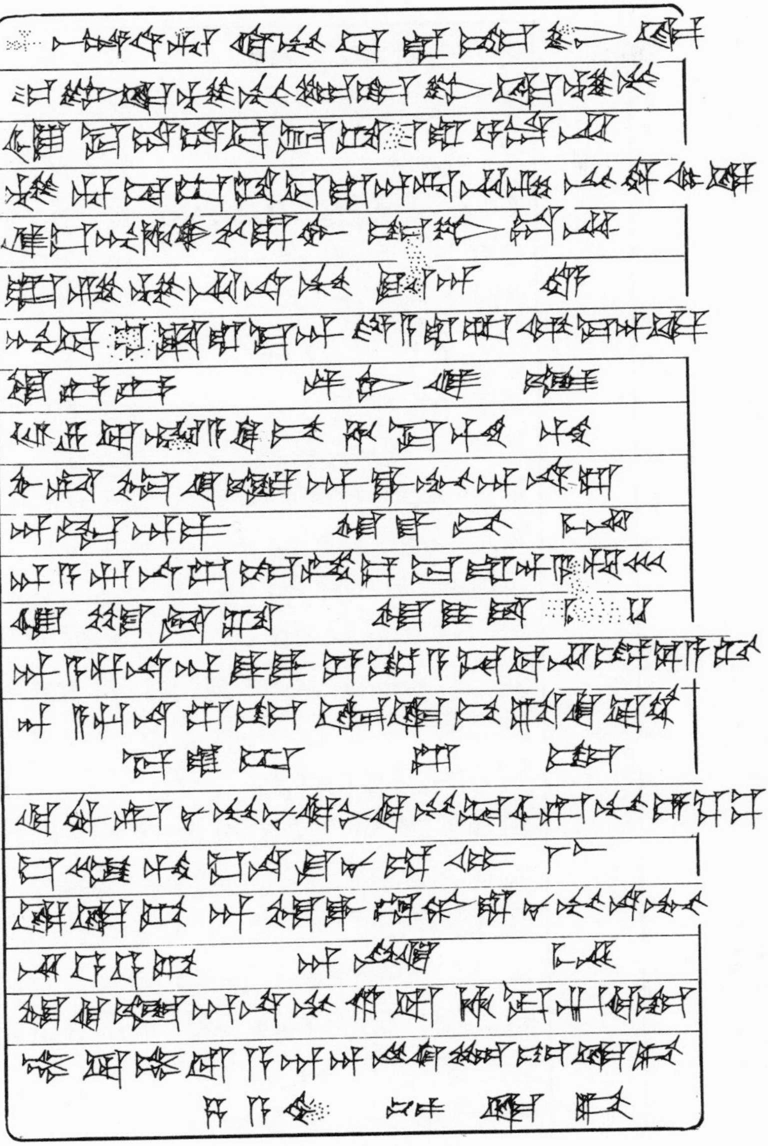

Plate 9   YBC 7167
Reverse

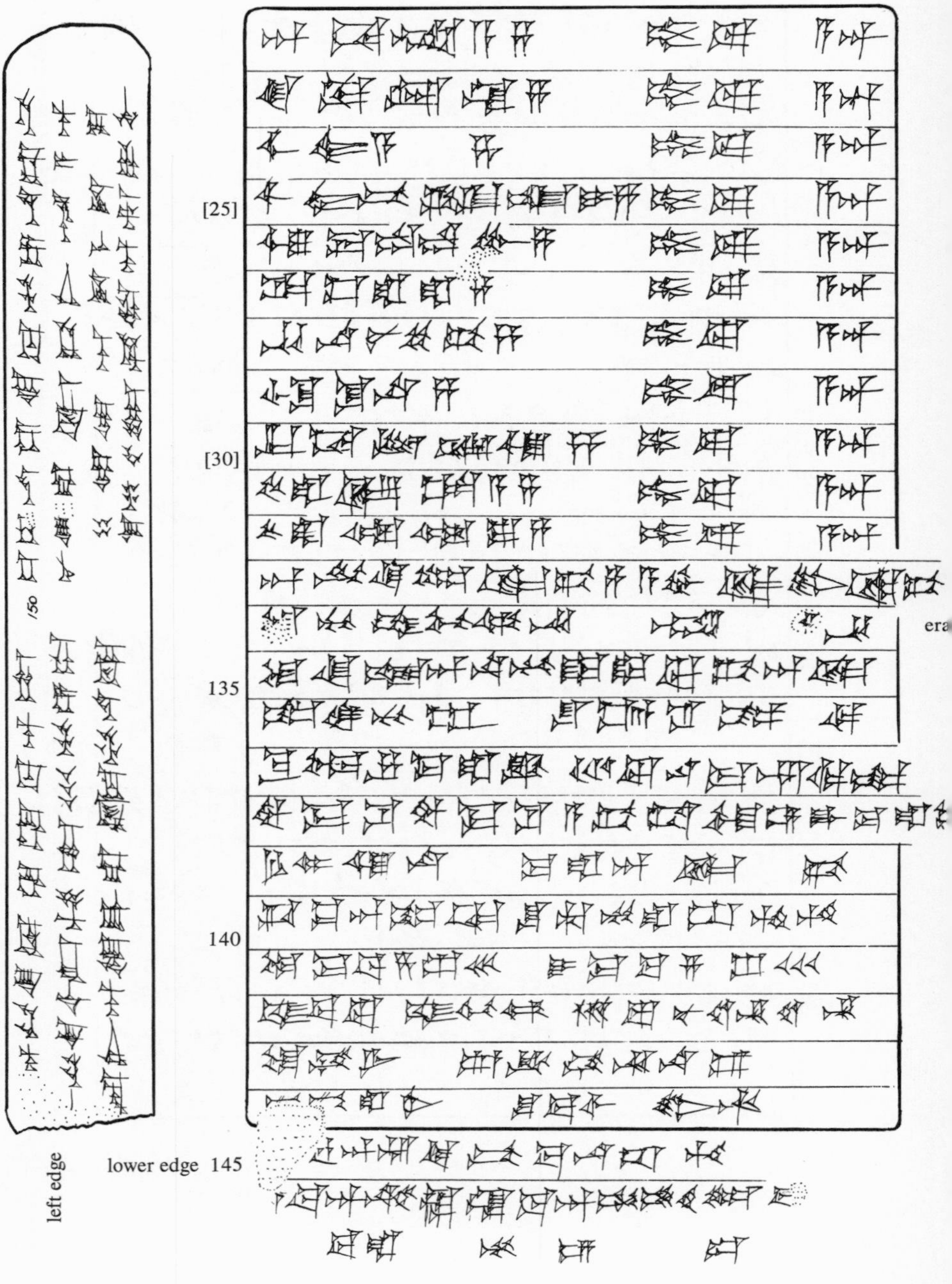

[25]

[30]

135

[135]

140

150

left edge

lower edge 145

era[sure]

Plate 10   YBC 4671
Obverse

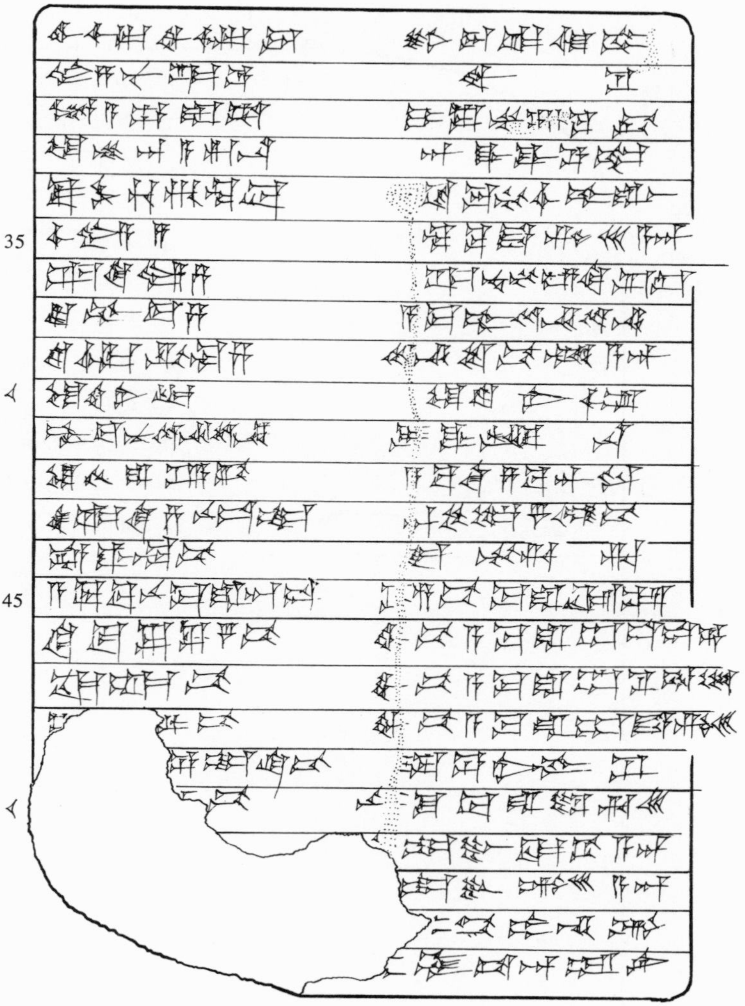

Plate 11   YBC 4671
Reverse

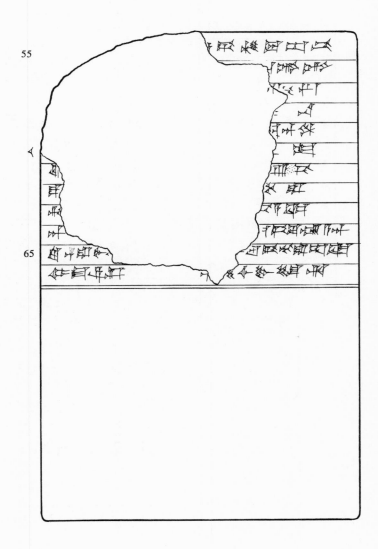

Plate 12 Collection A. Smit No. 10

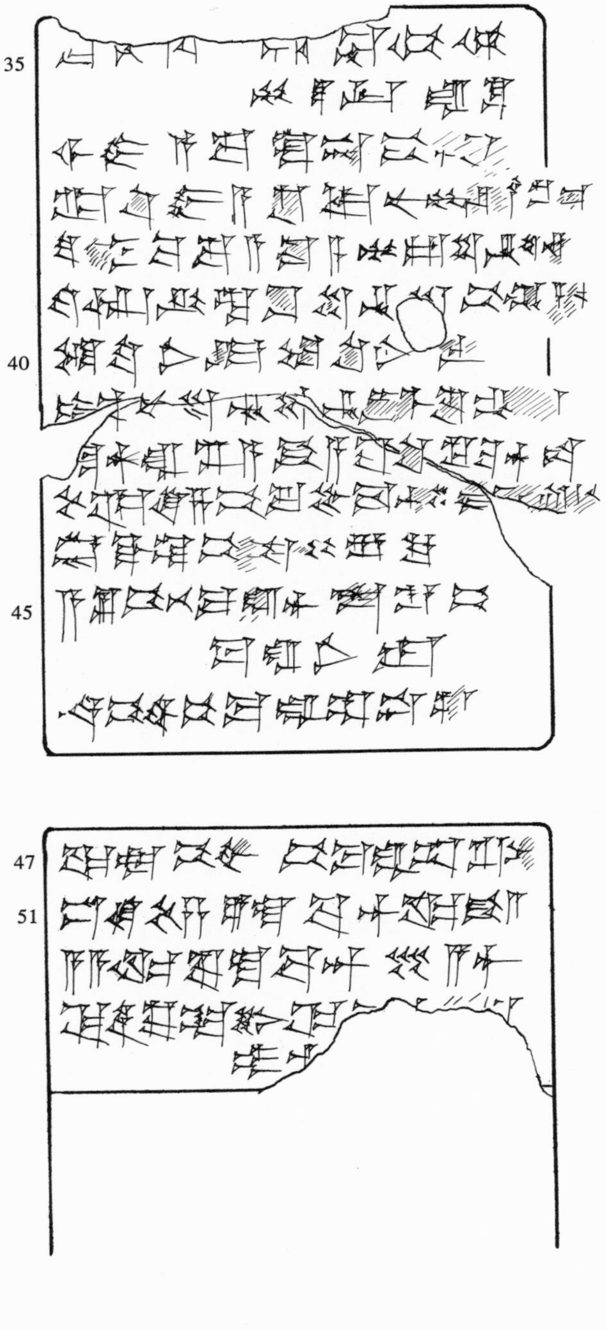